STENCIL
SOURCE BOOK 2

STENCIL
SOURCE BOOK 2
OVER 200 NEW DESIGNS

PATRICIA MEEHAN

NORTH LIGHT BOOKS

CINCINNATI, OHIO

First published in Great Britain in 1995 by
Anaya, Collins & Brown Limited, London

First published in North America
in 1995 by North Light Books,
an imprint of F&W Publications, Inc.
1507 Dana Avenue
Cincinnati, OH 45207
1-800/289-0963

1 3 5 7 9 8 6 4 2

Editor: Patsy North
Design: Sheila Volpe
Photography: Les Meehan (except those listed on page 144)
Charts and diagrams: Michael Volpe
Coral Mula

ISBN 0-89134-695-3

Typeset in Great Britain by Servis Filmsetting Limited, Manchester
Colour reproduced by Global Colour, Malaysia
Printed and bound in Italy

CONTENTS

INTRODUCTION

Welcome to the *Stencil Source Book 2*. I was very pleased to find that my first book was so popular, as I have been an enthusiastic stencil artist for many years now and I am always happy to seize any opportunity to pass this enthusiasm on to other people. Stencilling is a relaxing, satisfying and artistic hobby. It does not take long to learn and is tremendously rewarding. After reading this book and taking a little time to practise, you will be able to use your new-found talents almost anywhere. Your chosen projects can be quite large as in the field of home decoration or as small as ornamental trinket boxes.

People are often dismissive of stencilling, saying that they did stencilling at school and thought it rather a naïve art. When they see just what is possible today, they are absolutely astounded. The expertise of modern stencillers has raised the art form to new heights. With this book I hope to introduce the budding stencil artist to the delights of a new hobby and to spur on the dedicated stenciller with new designs and ideas. You do not have to be an artist to produce excellent results. There are so many wonderful stencils for you to buy and such a marvellous choice of paints available that you should have no difficulty in finding exactly what you want.

If you are new to stencilling, you should read the instructions at the back of the book before you make a start on any projects. If you have stencilled before, I urge you also to read the instructions. I make a point of reading the instructions in any stencilling book that I find. You never know what you may learn or indeed rediscover.

The book is divided into chapters based on themes, each containing lots of ideas to inspire you. At the end of each chapter, you will find a brand new collection of designs to copy. Some of these designs are very simple and hence easy to cut and use. Others are more complex. This does not mean that they are difficult to use. Once you are able to cut one hole cleanly from your stencil material, cutting more is just a matter of repetition. The same theory applies to the application of the colour. Once you have coloured in one hole, you can apply colour to them all.

Many of the designs from the book have been used and photographed in real-life situations. These are just suggestions for use and I would encourage you to be creative with the designs and imagine how they would appear in different colour combinations. This will give you confidence when you come to choose your own colour schemes. Try, too, tracing off your favourite designs and manipulating them to make different borders and motifs. This is not difficult and it will stimulate your design sense.

I hope that you will find much to enjoy in this second *Stencil Source Book*. It really is possible to learn how to stencil by reading a book. I did.

*With a few simple stencils, you can transform
any plain surface around your home.*

Chapter 1

KIDS' STUFF

*Fairy-tale castles and enchanted princesses;
galloping for miles on a friendly rocking
horse; playmates, pets and favourite toys;
picnics on long summer days. These are the
ingredients for a host of wonderful
childhood memories.*

I stencilled this nursery for a baby who was waiting to be born. The huge dancing frogs, teddy bears and rocking horses are placed at strategic points all around the room. A family of geese walks along the top of the skirting board at a level where a small baby crawling around can see them. The baby's father is a keen fisherman, so the little boy fishing was an ideal motif to use as a border.

A tiny, child-sized chair is enlivened with a mother goose and her train of goslings. Small bows add a darker contrast to the colour scheme.

I always enjoy stencilling a nursery more than any other room in the house. I try to create a happy, colourful room for a child to dream in. I can let my imagination run riot and go back, for however brief a span, to imagining myself a child again. Because you can stencil directly onto the wall, the decorations you make for your young child can easily be painted over as the child grows older. You can then stencil again with a new design more suitable to your child's current age and tastes. If you have two children sharing a room, each half of the room can be personalized with different designs and stencilled names appropriate to each child.

I am still a great believer in educational stencilling. Fat, juicy caterpillars ambling around the wall can have letters (see pages 128 and 129) or numbers stencilled into their segments. Use a different colour for each caterpillar or even each segment if you can. Try to colour just around the edges of the segments. This will give outlines to the shapes and leave the centres clear for the letters. You will then be able to change the contents at regular intervals without disturbing the main caterpillar design. For added interest, you can show each caterpillar biting into a different piece of fruit or use the lettering to spell out your child's name.

Animals are always a great favourite with children. Farm animals, especially, are very traditional and easily recognized by the young. They can be accompanied by fences, fields, trees and farm buildings. Donkeys are popular and can be stencilled walking, running, kicking or just refusing to move. Stencil a single donkey on the wall minus its tail. Then stencil a tail onto a piece of card and you have the simple childhood game of "pin the tail on the donkey".

For something a little different, try using wild animals to create a mini-jungle. Lion, tiger and giraffe heads peering through half-parted foliage would make an exciting border. Each animal head could be used again for spot decoration elsewhere around the room. Of course, there are many other animals to choose from. The same idea could be tried with birds on leafy branches with bright tropical flowers or using fish in watery settings. You could even stencil a different number of colourful bubbles rising from each fish's mouth.

Space is another area that captures the imagination of the young. Stars and planets stencilled on the ceiling are not a new idea. However, if you combine this with coloured rockets flying up the walls, you will add a whole new dimension to the décor. Use one set of rockets on the wall in a vertical line, diminishing in size as they climb, and you can create a really unusual height chart. As your child grows, add a space-walking astronaut to each rocket he reaches.

This bright toy-box was first painted cream. The lid and base were then sponged with green paint and the centre panel sponged with yellow. Paint effects always give a wonderful depth to stencilling. The teddy bear design on the lid has been slightly adapted by the addition of a set of juggling balls in different colours.

Take a step into a fairy-tale where thorny briars wander around the walls. A pretty pink, green and blue colour scheme is just perfect for this little girl's bedroom.

Children are always fascinated by other children, so why not stencil some playmates for your child to talk to? You can dress them in very bright clothes, changing the colours at each repeat, or in clothes to match your child's wardrobe. There are several designs of children at the end of this chapter. If you enlarge them, you can add other details such as extra facial features or patterns on the clothing. Don't be afraid to stencil large designs on your child's walls. Larger-than-life teddies

and dolls, birds or animals are easily accepted in a child's make-believe world, especially if you clothe them.

It would not be too difficult to create a special woodland scene. Grasses, ferns and small trees can be inhabited by small furry animals such as mice, rabbits and moles. This may sound rather ambitious, but if you design the scene bit by bit it will soon build up into something wonderful. A garden scene would be another project idea. Clumps of flowers growing around the wall at

skirting-board height, with grasses and maybe a bird-table, would not be difficult. You could add bees, butterflies, ladybirds and perhaps a cat asleep in the grass.

There are many simpler schemes or small touches to add to your child's room. What about a candlestick complete with candle next to the bed? Colour the flame with fluorescent paint to glow in the faintest light. A small fairy could hover over the bed to guard your child in the darkness. Between you, you can name the fairy and make up stories about her at bedtime. If your child has a favourite animal and, for one reason or another, you cannot have pets, you can stencil the animal onto the wall. Again, it can be named and talked to, and will not have to be fed or taken for a walk. Maybe your child wants something unsuitable as a pet; my niece, for instance, wanted an earthworm. With stencilling, no problem.

Monsters are not to be ruled out. Many children have a fondness for them, as they are still part of the make-believe world and as such are not threatening. Alternatively, you could create a helicopter cockpit over the bedhead or a mountain scene complete with misty clouds and rainbows.

The first source of inspiration when stencilling for the slightly older child will be the child's own preferences. Perhaps your child could also join in with the actual decoration of the room. Youngsters are always fond of deciding what is their favourite colour in the whole wide world.

Children's own drawings can provide you with some unique inspiration, too, and can form the basis of your stencil designs. Colour schemes can be bright and vibrant or pale and pastel. The choice is yours, or your child's. One thing is certain: your child will have an original, interesting room in which to while away the hours.

In this close-up of the stencilling, you can see Sleeping Beauty's turretted castle with flags flying.

This old-fashioned bench seat and desk were treated to a coat of dark blue paint, then over-painted in a pale grey-blue. It was then sanded back in places to allow the darker blue to show through. The final stencilling continues the Sleeping Beauty theme.

Sleeping Beauty's castle surrounded by briars is delightful in a little girl's bedroom. Use it on a toy-box or for curtains and bedding. Place the Sleeping Beauty figure from page 16 around the walls or in door panels.

The falling stars are ideal to mix with the fairytale stencils. Colour the stars in pastel shades or make them as vibrant as fireworks by using bright metallic paints.

The three fairytale figures shown here – Sleeping Beauty, Cinderella, and her fairy godmother – can be used with the castle on pages 14 and 15.

A rocking horse is perfect for stencilling around a wall. Vary the angle of the horse so that it appears to rock backwards and forwards as it gallops along.

The little boy with his fishing rod could be stencilled on the wall just above a chest of drawers with a really long fishing line down to the floor, while the simple ballerina can pirouette on a bedhead in a little girl's bedroom. Try the geese and goslings on a bedhead, too.

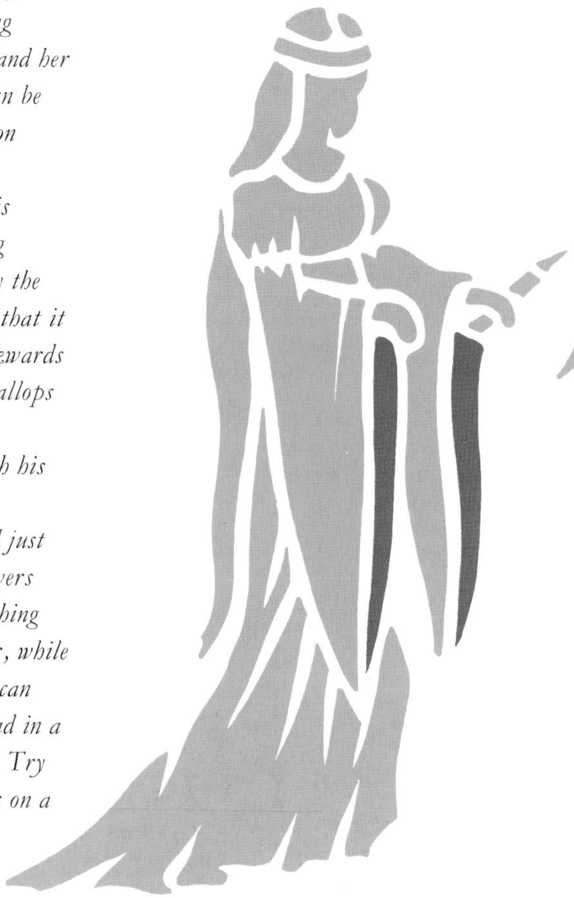

The simple teddy has to be cut using two overlays, one for the body and one for the eyes and other details. Stencil him large on a baby's bed cover or on a cotton mat for the nursery floor. The dancing frog is singing in the rain. Use lots of bright colours, changing them as you go, to make a stunning wall border. You could then add the design to a laundry bag with the child's name. Again, cut a separate overlay for the details.

The ladybird is a pretty motif for a young child's chair or curtains, or it could be made to march along the skirting board. The little girl with her dog and the little boy can be paired up to make a lively border in a shared playroom.

Chapter 2

CLEAN LINES

Greek columns; triangles, pyramids and cones; geometric shapes, stripes and cubes; zigzag lightning and angled desk lamps; crystals and fine white china. You can make very effective stencils using only simple classical shapes.

PREVIOUS PAGE Box-shaped plant pot holders are ideal projects for stencilling. These examples have been colour-washed and then dry-brushed with gold enamel paint. The gold was then repeated in one of the simple stencil designs, while the other was worked in blue.

A classical Greek key stencil is the perfect design to complement this simply styled room. It is coloured in a restful green and, surprisingly, shaded with purple.

There is no doubt that most of the designs in this section will look at their best in modern houses or houses that themselves have clean lines. However, if you live in an old house, you can still use them as long as they please you and don't look out of place. The one big advantage of stencilling is that you make all the choices. Of course, you can go and buy rolls of wallpaper and lengths of fabric, but with stencilling you can use your own designs to co-ordinate your house.

Now, what can you use for subject matter? Look at Art Deco books, where you will find lots of designs in a simple, uncluttered style to fit the bill exactly.

Look at Sixties' style with its geometric patterns or Greek architecture with its classical columns. There are many subjects, such as people's faces, that look wonderful in silhouette. So trace around some interesting pictures and see what you can come up with. It may be that, as a silhouette, your subject does not work too well and may be quite unrecognizable, but you may still have found a wonderful shape from which to make a stencil.

Use Arabic, Cyrillic or Chinese scripts to make swirling patterns full of movement. Coloured with shades of blue and turquoise, they could give a wave-like effect in a cream-painted

bathroom. Ribbons may sound too fussy a subject for this section, but you can create a very effective border made up of simple bows. In a bedroom with otherwise plain decoration, it would give a touch of femininity and soften otherwise-stark lines. The colour you use would also change the effect. Think how different it would look in either salmon pink or navy blue or perhaps a mixture of the two colours.

In the 'Materials and Techniques' section at the end of the book, you will see some designs based on just one tulip motif (see pages 140–141). To take this idea one step further, choose two or three simple geometric shapes and see how many different borders and motifs you can make with them. Try a long, thin rectangle, a small circle and a square to start with and then try other

combinations of shapes. You could use small cut-out pieces of coloured felt for this exercise. I promise that you will enjoy yourself and the time will simply fly by. Many of the simple designs you create in this way would make perfect borders around other stencils. They could enclose floral borders, for instance, on walls and floors. You could use them on picture frames or mounts (mats) and around doorways.

Take a look at some books on modern art or go to exhibitions if you can. What seem like simplistic shapes can really be masterpieces of composition. The relationship between the colours and shapes is what counts. Find a book on colour theory and see which are the dominant or receding colours. This will be enjoyable and will help your colour sense.

Three stencilled terracotta pots were first painted white, then colourwashed. This is an easy treatment and pots make a simple project for you to try.

The simple sticks border can be manipulated quite easily to make lots of different shapes. Here it makes pyramids along the wall, but you could use it to make panels as well.

There are many dried floral wreaths made by attaching flowers to twig circlets. I recently decorated a bedroom and used several of these circlets as the basis for the scheme interspersed with simple berries. In the kitchen, basic fruit designs are ideal. You can colour them in with blocks of solid colour or use shading to give them shape. Apples, figs and oranges are all effective. You could use grapes, too, but for a change, square off all the fruit and leaf shapes. This would give a really interesting effect if you stencilled it as a border. Also, because the design would be more like a mosaic, it would lose its specific kitchen look and could then be used anywhere else in the house. Other leaf shapes would fit this brief and could be made to twist and trail around the room. For the bathroom, simple

fish shapes or boats in a border or on curtains would be perfect. Use brilliant colours to make them stand out from the walls.

Ovals can be in any size and can be used in a horizontal or vertical position. Make a border of horizontal ovals for your hallway and use clever shading to give them shape. You could put a device such as a small square or dot in between or inside each shape.

Mosaic shapes make effective stencils. You can turn almost any subject into a mosaic. Flowers, birds and fish are ideal. Mosaic letters on the hall floor would make an unusual welcome mat. Or use numerals to put a date on the outside of your house.

Take a look at stained glass windows, both ancient and modern. The images are already broken down into segments and, as such, are perfectly adaptable into stencil designs. Many other objects have clean lines. Racing cars, ocean-going liners, the New York skyline and golf clubs are just a few. All of these would be ideal designs for a masculine environment.

Early American decoration is another area where you can find a clean, simplistic approach to design. Naïve flowers, trees and fruits abound and would be at home today in an uncluttered environment. Swedish folk art is very traditional and you can create stencils in this style to give your furniture a country feel. Tribal art from Africa or Australia can consist of quite complex interwoven patterns, but will have the basic clean lines and shapes from which to construct your own designs.

Colour plays an important role when working with clean-edged designs. If you have opted for an ethnic look, try to use traditional colours for authenti-

city. Early American designs look at their best in the colours that were available at the time rather than, say, shocking pink and metallics.

Cross stitch embroidery also simplifies shapes. Either look at embroidery patterns for inspiration or create your own embroideries based on stencil designs. You could stencil a scene or sampler directly onto evenweave fabric or canvas for a fire screen, for example. Something of this size would not be too daunting for the beginner. The stencilled motifs can then be embroidered over or can be left unworked as you wish.

Patchwork would not seem to be suitable subject matter for this chapter, but, if you look at the shapes and ignore the patterned fabrics, the geometric repeat designs will leap out at you. So take a fresh look at your surroundings and the familiar articles in your home and I am sure you will find lots of ideas to prompt your designing skills.

These bold African figures stand out sharply from the wall. Their bright clothing and shields add punch to a simple design.

The Greek key is a very popular design and exists in many forms. It is elegant, simple and classical. It can be used almost anywhere and in any colours you choose. You can introduce lots of colours to the chevron design for a rainbow effect or, if you like your decoration a little more subdued, use gradations of just one colour. You will get a different effect if you use the darkest colour for the straight-edged element than if you use it in the centre.

I am rather fond of the swirls. Using the pattern randomly all over a chimney-breast would give the effect of rough plaster. It also looks rather like a minimalist wave, which would be striking stencilled in blues in a white bathroom. Chunky wedges in pastel shades could decorate a bed or the wall around the bedhead.

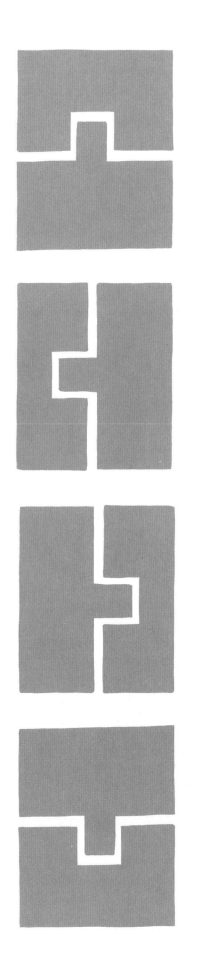

For a wonderful three-dimensional effect, stencil the front portion of the pincers design in, say, pale grey and the back portion in black. It would look effective in a modern hallway or along a landing, repeated along the edge of curtains. The commas are extremely simple to cut. Try them in gold on black around a mirror in a sophisticated living room.

The bundles can be rotated as you go along and would make a jewel-bright border around a fireplace or on bedding.

The interlocking squares are made up of one design rotated through 360 degrees. You can try this method with many other designs too.

I just love the African herdsmen with their setting sun. They would make a stunning wall border, especially in a modern sitting room. Changing the colours of the robes at each repeat will have extra impact.

The sticks design reminds me of cinnamon, but can be stencilled using any colours. For a clean, fresh-looking kitchen, use blue or green and for a bright bathroom use yellow and green.

The shield designs can be used in many combinations to create wall borders or motifs. They would also be suitable on cushions or an ethnic throw for your sofa. Either bright or earth colours would be suitable. The warrior can be added at intervals to a border with the shield designs, but do reverse the figure every now and then for added interest.

HINT OF SPRING

Crocuses peeping out of the slowly warming soil; drifts of daffodils bringing sunshine to the garden; the first butterflies of the year; pale blue skies and shy buds appearing on the trees. It is wonderful to be alive on an early spring day with the sun giving a promise of the year to come.

PREVIOUS PAGE Spring flowers are just one idea for you to stencil onto stationery to add your own personal style.

A hint of spring on a cold winter's night. The flickering candle in this bright holder will cast a glowing, warm light onto these delicate lily of the valley stems.

An unusual alcove has been given a touch of style with a pretty floral motif that repeats the colours in the striped wallpaper.

Spring is an absolutely marvellous time of year. You can almost feel the excitement in the air as flowers start to bloom, birds start to sing and the world wakes up from a winter's sleep. Every new flower found in the garden is a small miracle to be shared with family or friends. Each individual crocus is just as beautiful as a whole carpet of the flowers under the trees. Many spring flowers are bright as if to make up for the colour starvation of the winter months.

You only have to look around the countryside, public parks and your own garden to find your inspiration for springtime motifs. Stencil some little plant pots above the tiles in your kitchen. They are simple shapes and easy to cut. Then make yourself a selection of stencils of hyacinths, violets and primroses to fill the pots. You can also make one larger pot and put all three flowers inside.

*A brightly stencilled
tablecloth adds life to this
sitting room. The anemones
are strongly coloured, with
just one flower picking out
the colour in the sofa.*

Look at the flowering trees as well. A border of magnolias in your sitting room would be lovely and you can carry the design onto cupboard doors or door panels. Cherry blossom is beautiful too. Stencil branches of it onto the edges of curtains and scatter single flowers onto the walls.

Camellias can be difficult to grow in the garden, but you can make stencilled bushes grow out of stencilled pots in the house where they don't have to battle against sharp frosts. The flowers normally come in a wide variety of colours from red to pink to lavender, but you can choose your own colours to fit into any room. Try putting a single large plant as a focal point in a bathroom or in a conservatory. This will look really spectacular.

Tablecloths are very good surfaces on which to try out your stencilling skills. Use spring flowers on a large cream tablecloth. You can then be adventurous and make three more, stencilling them with summer, autumn and winter themes.

Design yourself a wicker flower basket and fill it with stencilled pansies. This would look attractive positioned on the wall just above a hall table. Place real pansies in a small vase on the table and let them intermingle with your blooms. Never be afraid to put something in front of your stencilling. I have stencilled large plants onto people's walls and am never upset if they hang a picture on the same wall. Stencilling is just a backdrop for you and your family to live with.

This suburban hallway is long and narrow. Touches of stencilling here and there are just enough to give it style without being overpowering.

I recently asked a friend of ours what came into his mind when he thought of spring. He said, "Birds singing." I foolishly replied that I could not stencil those, and he immediately suggested stencilled birds with musical notes pouring from their beaks. What a wayward idea, but why not! Choose a bird and your favourite music too!

Another unusual idea is to buy some inexpensive straw hats and stencil both inside and outside the brim with spring flowers. Add lashings of ribbon and silk flowers and you will have a pretty selection of hats to last you through the spring and summer. If you have children, you can stencil matching hats for them too. Canvas bags, T-shirts and skirts can all be given the treatment.

Stencil them in the winter months and cheer up the dark evenings with thoughts of spring.

There are lots of small items you can stencil as gifts or for sale in spring fêtes. Pot-pourri bags, handkerchiefs, vases and plant pots, stationery and little boxes are just a few ideas to spur you on. For the kitchen you could decorate utensil jars, labels for home-made jams and beaded drinks covers.

What about stencilling a row of playful lambs in a child's nursery? They could be leaping in the air, sniffing flowers or even jumping fences. One extra-large lamb could stand on the bedhead or the side of the cot. Of course, bedding could then be made to match the décor.

You could create a pretty collection of spring flowers on a chest of drawers. Place a larger circlet or oval of flowers on the top with sprigs of flowers on the drawers. Use a mixture of bluebells, narcissi and wood anemones in the circlet. Then use bluebell motifs on the top drawer, narcissi on the next one down and so on.

Pale yellow bedroom walls with a border of deeper yellow daffodils would make waking up each morning a pleasure. Pale green walls scattered with motifs of the palest pink wood anemones would be a peaceful decorative scheme for a guest room. The same motif carried onto pine bedroom furniture and a lampshade would add the finishing touches.

Apple blossom covers the orchards in a pinky-white froth in springtime. This is a beautiful flower that would also look charming in a bedroom. Treat yourself to some bed hangings. You do not have to have a four-poster bed to make your bedroom look really special. Use swathes of fine lawn or butter muslin (cheesecloth) draped from a central point on the wall over the bed. There are many different ways to drape the fabric; you can get ideas from interior decorating books and magazines. Stencil the hangings with apple blossom and make sheer curtains to match, then cut corner piece motifs and stencil them into the top corners of the walls. Pale flowers and green leaves with brown branches as a contrast would be a very natural colour scheme and would not be overpowering.

A visit to the local garden centre or a winter's evening spent browsing through seed catalogues and natural history books would be very enjoyable methods of seeking out sources for your own spring flower designs.

Pretty yellow polyanthus plants decorate a painted window-box brimming with colourful flowers.

Bluebells are a childhood favourite. Use masses of them along the wall at skirting-board level for an unusual border in a little girl's bedroom. Look at the design from different angles and you will find many ways to use it.

The spring bow, if reduced on a photocopier, would look really lovely on a picture mount (mat) or around the edge of a small table. In the wild the violet grows purple or white. Use the purple form on a white-painted dressing table and the white flowers on a black jewellery box. The little daisy would look delightful on net curtains or on navy blue muslin (cheesecloth) to be used as bed hangings.

The crocus provides a
carpet of colour in the
springtime, so why not use
this design on a floorcloth.
They are easy to make and
very durable. The fragile
beauty of the lily of the
valley is without equal.
Imagine how this would
look stencilled onto a glass
lampshade or on a glass
door panel.

Anemones are one of my
favourite flowers. Their
depth and variety of colour
is astonishing. This design
of anemones, tulip and
leaves is very versatile and
can be executed in both
vivid and pastel colours.
Use it to brighten up an
old tray or a plain vase.

The peony run is very
adaptable. See how many
different arrangements you
can create from it. The
complete design can be used
as a border around the
walls with smaller elements
as isolated motifs.

This daffodil would be very attractive running around a doorway. Don't forget to reverse the design halfway around the frame. If you don't, the flowers will be upside down on one half and will look odd. Pretty forget-me-nots are extremely delicate flowers. This border will look best on small pieces of furniture or winding its way along a dado rail.

Polyanthus come in all sorts of bright colours. Stencil them in a row in the kitchen. To make them really cheerful, change the colour of the petals at each repeat. Make some cushions for your garden chairs and stencil each of them with a different colour of petal for each member of the family.

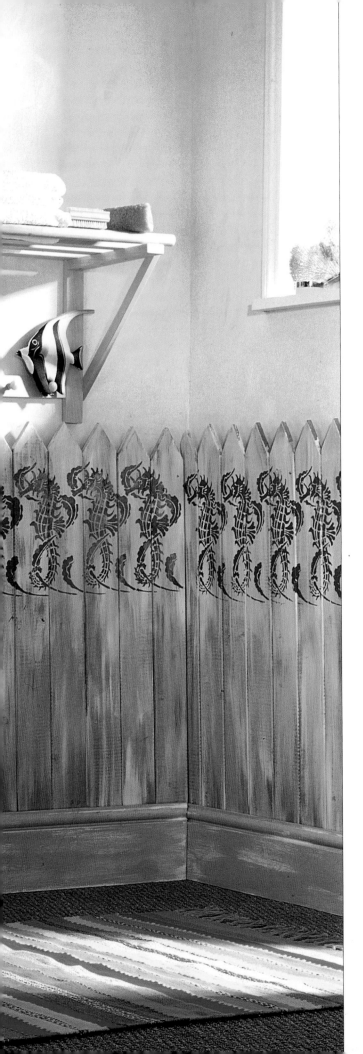

Chapter 4

WATER'S EDGE

Tide pools filled with shells; the pattern of the waves on the shore; lilies floating on the tranquil surface of a pool; a fountain gurgling in the evening light. Water has so many moods and can be the most calming of the elements.

PREVIOUS PAGE *Stencilled sea-horses make an eye-catching feature on the wooden panelling running around this cheerful bathroom.*

This is a combination of two stencils from page 53, the galleon and the fish and anchors. They provide a touch of whimsy in this practical bathroom.

Sea shells are a favourite bathroom design. They look pretty stencilled in realistic colours, but why not try really bright colours like the ones shown here?

What immediately springs to mind when you think of the water's edge? Is it the sea-shore, a river bank or maybe a swimming pool? I think of a small pond in the countryside with rushes and darting dragonflies.

Of course, a bathroom is the first place you would think of as the setting for a watery decorative theme, so we will start there.

Sea shells come in a vast array of shapes and sizes. Because they are segmented, they make ideal subjects for stencilling. Metallic gold or pearlized sea shells stencilled in a border onto green sponged walls would be an exciting bathroom feature. Use a mixture of different shells for variety. You could add the shells as motifs on sheer voile curtains and on the sides of the bath. Design some exotic fish and stencil them on a cotton rug for the bathroom floor. You can use really bright colours or pastel, pearlized paints, as either would look delightful.

A border of miniature desert islands would be amusing around the top of the bath. Make them slightly different sizes and vary the number of palm trees as you go. You could also add clouds, seagulls or flying fish to the border at intervals. The odd shark's fin would give a touch of humour to the subject.

Dolphins are another classic watery subject and could be stencilled in groups on your bathroom floor. Mermaids are also a fun subject. They can sit on rocks combing their hair or swim in an underwater kingdom. For a modern approach, stencil a row of windsurfers in the bathroom. The sails are always dazzlingly bright, so you can go to town with the colour scheme.

There are many different water birds to use for inspiration. Ducks could be stencilled in your hallway, flying in formation over tall bulrushes. Herons, geese and bright pink flamingoes are all suitable for inclusion in this chapter. A stand of large flamingoes would look marvellous as a centrepiece in your bathroom, or single birds could be added to just a few of the tiles.

Water is ideally blue or green and these are the perfect calming colours for a bedroom. Set aside one small corner of your bedroom and in it stencil a small fountain with water cascading into a pool. This is not as difficult as it sounds. Many garden fountains are very simple in design and can be easily converted into a stencil. Water is just arched, wavy lines and tear-shaped droplets. Finish your work with a few jewel-bright water lilies floating on the surface of the pond. You could carry the theme over onto a blanket chest, if you have one. These pieces of furniture are absolutely marvellous for the stenciller. They are not too big for a beginner to take on, and yet they offer great scope to the more experienced stenciller. The flat top surface is ideal for a set central motif that can be edged with a co-ordinating border if you choose.

Exotic fish brighten up these plain tiles. If you want to practise before you embark on a large project such as a bathroom, try stencilling single tiles to use as hot-plate mats for the kitchen or dining room.

Try to find interesting boxes to stencil. I picked this one up for a song, sanded off the original decoration, and added my own. This is for my sister-in-law who collects froggy things. I will decorate another with flowers in the panels for myself.

In the kitchen you will find more surfaces for your endeavours. Bright-eyed kingfishers can perch on leafy branches and look down on your work surface, while others can swoop down to the sink. They are the most beautiful birds with their turquoise and orange plumage. If you live near the sea, you could stencil your kitchen walls with simple fishing boats, lobsters and creels or pretty sea anemones.

To give your stencilling a nautical feel, look at a book about knot-tying. You will find knots ranging from the simple to the complex, all of which are easy to convert into stencils, as each twist of the rope becomes a separate segment. You can use several knots to make up one border, or stencil a small collection of knots onto the wall and then stencil a frame around them. This would be an ideal way to introduce

stencilling into a masculine environment. You could also make elegant rope swags and loops and stencil them as an imitation handrail along your hallway and up the stairs.

Old sailing ships are wonderful subjects for stencilling. Make an extra-large ship with billowing sails, use it to decorate the chimney breast and then encircle it with stencilled ship's wheels. Turn the ship into a pirate galleon anchored off a desert island for a child's playroom. You could incorporate an old treasure map as well, with the four winds blowing from the corners and dolphins and sea monsters in the waves. Old-fashioned divers in diving suits would be fun to stencil for children, too, especially if you added colourful fish and a treasure chest to the sea bed. There are many other nautical themes for you to try, such as compasses, flags and nets complete with coloured glass weights.

In your dining room you could design a border of reeds and rushes interspersed with waterside wildlife such as otters, frogs and dragonflies resting on arched grasses. The dragonflies, with their brilliant blue and red colourings, could also be added to a glass pendant light over the table. Swans swimming in a line, leaving a trail of ripples in their wake, would make a tasteful border that could be stencilled onto a dark tablecloth and a set of matching napkins.

There are many sources of reference from which to seek out your designs. Books on sea birds, fresh and sea-water fish, and water gardening are just a few. Try books on ships and boats of the world as well. Colour schemes can be as restful or as vibrant as you wish. Use cool greens for ferns and foliage, deep blues and turquoise for the sea and creams or reds for ships' sails. Glass is a wonderful surface for stencils as, like water, it is transparent and will add a new dimension to your work. The water's edge is an exciting theme with a rainbow of colours to choose from.

The kingfisher makes a bright and cheerful addition to this house sign. You can easily make your own original sign with just numbers or by illustrating the name of your house.

49

Cut an extra overlay for the shaded parts of these curved sea shells. They would make a magnificent floor border in your bathroom in pastel shades or could be stencilled at random on the bath surround in metallic gold. The mermaid is another fun design. Change the colour of her hair at every repeat and use pearlized paints for her tail.

The Chinese wave (below) would make a simple basis for an oriental scheme. Use it on a dark background with blue water and white or cream foam.

The scallops and swirls (opposite) are extremely elegant and would look good as a border at picture rail height in a hallway.

Use the sturdy galleon as a motif on the wall at each end of your bath. It would look equally good in bright colours or more subdued shades. Make brightly coloured fish in metallic or iridescent paints swim around the anchors and chain. Combine the fish and the octopus with the mermaid (page 50) and anchor stencils for an interesting frieze. The palm tree can be used either as a simple motif or as a border with its little island and patch of ocean.

A bright pink flamingo could stand guard on each side of your bathroom mirror, while the fat frog, blended in shades of green, can be used as a fun motif near the sink or the bath taps. The swan is very elegant and can be stencilled onto a cotton mat or the glass of a bathroom cabinet. The oranges and blues of the kingfisher are beautiful to see; stencil this bird perched high on the bathroom walls.

The pond with reeds is a simple stencil design that would look very effective running along the wall just above the bath, while the stylized border of waves and fish is just begging to be used around a bathroom mirror or as an edging to tiles and curtains.

Chapter 5

FLORAL DANCE

*Fields of poppies; clematis cascading
around a doorway and daisies in a jam-jar;
a patchwork of Dutch bulb fields and
meadows starred with wild flowers.
Flowers are everywhere and have been a
favourite motif for artists and craftsmen
throughout the centuries.*

PREVIOUS PAGE *Three useful little boxes have been given the stencil treatment. You can make the stencil decoration really lavish on items such as these and give them as gifts. Match the decoration to the occasion.*

Peach-coloured flowers, yellow ribbon and green leaves combine to create a co-ordinated bedroom.

Almost everyone loves flowers. They come in so many shapes and sizes that it would be difficult not to find one to please. For inspiration, look at different flower shapes in a gardening book. Look, too, at art history books and notice the difference between, for example, flowers in the Art Nouveau and the Art Deco styles. There are dainty flowers such as the scarlet pimpernel; flamboyant lilies and cacti; multi-petalled, full-blown roses; trailing flowers such as fuchsias and others that turn their faces upwards to the sun.

You can build up a co-ordinated floral scheme quite easily. Pick your favourite flower and make a simple stencil of the bloom. Add a few leaves and you have created your first basic motif. Make it a little more complex by adding a few more blooms, facing in different directions, perhaps, or some partially hidden behind the others. (Try to use an odd number of flowers and leaves. This will always look compositionally better than an even number.) To make a border design, add some ribbon and use this element to join two motifs

together. By enlarging, reducing and reversing the same flower and leaf patterns, you can create quite a complex swag design. This is how I designed the dog rose selection in the trace-off patterns at the end of this chapter and you can see how effective they are in the bedroom photographs. The client wanted a warm colour scheme in her favourite shades of peach and yellow. Try to imagine the same design in your favourite colours, perhaps red roses with pink ribbon, blue roses with turquoise ribbon or gold flowers with white ribbon on a dark background.

I decorated walls, bedding and fitted wardrobes for my client, but there are many other surfaces to choose from in a bedroom. A lampshade decorated inside and out, curtains, pelmets (valances), or a quilted cotton rug for the floor are just a few examples. You could also consider dressing-tables, chests, bedroom chairs and door panels. Your bedroom slippers and night clothes might also enter the scheme. Of course, I will now add my usual words of caution. Please do not attempt to use all these ideas in one room. You will simply overdo it and be disappointed with the end result.

If you are an experienced needle-worker, a really worthwhile project would be a bedspread with quilting around a stencilled design. A smaller project would be to quilt a set of stencilled cushion covers.

Floral designs can be used all around the house. Although they are often more popular with women than men, they can be made acceptable by the use of more "masculine" colour schemes. These could include dusty pink and dark green, navy blue and burnt orange or perhaps green and gold. Black flowers with grey leaves are quite stunning too. Change the floral shape by making it stylized or interpreting it as a mosaic.

The stencil border design has been used to make the motifs on these fitted wardrobes, which now co-ordinate beautifully with the bedroom.

Different elements of the border stencil have been enlarged, reduced or reversed to build up this beautiful motif. It is a simple idea for you to try with your own stencils.

This pretty little window in a country cottage has a beautiful view but not much sunlight. The landing has been brightened up by this trailing floral motif.

Leaves, stems and petals are ideal design material. As they are easy to divide up into segments, they can be readily adapted to stencilling. Think about where you find flowers growing. There are small flowers that hug the ground in clumps and giant sunflowers that seem to reach to the sky. Some flowers trail along the ground, while others climb walls and fences to tumble over pergolas. Take your imagination one step further and you will see that stencilled flowers on your walls, floors and ceilings can be a decorative feature in direct imitation of nature.

If you have wooden floors, you can stencil a carpet of flowers anywhere in the house. This would be particularly pretty in a small girl's room or perhaps in a conservatory. A sinuous border of lilies trailing along the edges of your hall floor, then continuing up the staircase and along the landing would be extremely elegant. You could change the colour of the flowers to match the colour schemes in each different area.

With free-style designs you can build up a cascade of flowers starting from the ceiling, then tumbling over doorways and windows to the floor. You can use almost any stencil in a free-style manner. Just take individual elements and build up the stencilling as you go along. Look at the grape design and its use in Chapter 10 and you will soon get the idea. Stencil flowers around your windows and make some of them look as though they are growing in from the outside. If you are lucky enough to have shutters, they are an ideal surface on which to practise your talents. You may have a plain glass panel in your front door. Don't pay for expensive stained glass; just give it the stencil treatment. Alternatively, decorate a translucent muslin (cheesecloth) curtain with scattered sprigs of wild flowers in soft colours. This will look delicate and pretty at the window, while giving you privacy or hiding a less-than-perfect view.

In your kitchen you can use a simple floral design in a monochrome colour scheme. A small flower and leaf pattern in plain Wedgwood blue, green or pink would be very pretty. Try enclosing each motif in a stencilled square for a tile effect. If you sponge or rag roll the walls first in a slightly paler shade of your chosen colour, you will add an extra dimension to the decoration.

It would be an interesting concept to base your stencil designs around "collections". Shakespeare's flowers, mountain flowers, flowers particular to your own region are just a few ideas to set you thinking. Buy a diary with one page for each day and stencil a different flower for each one. You could also make your own stationery and calling cards.

One special little touch would be to match your pot-pourri to your decoration. Stencil roses on the walls and have rose-scented pot-pourri in the room. You could stencil cushions with lavender and fill them with the same dried herb. These would make pretty gifts for friends on special occasions.

Make your own carpet of flowers by stencilling your favourite blooms onto a floor cloth.

Add a touch of luxury to your life with these two dog rose and ribbon designs. Use them in a bedroom or in a sunny sitting room. They will work together in many ways. The large swag looks wonderful on cupboard doors or in a group of four radiating out from the centre of a round table. The smaller design can be used as a border interspersed with the swag or alone around a window frame. Try using different elements of the designs to make up some more co-ordinating stencil patterns.

You can almost see the tulips blowing in the breeze. Cut out two stencils, one reversed, and run the design around your fireplace.

This large floral design (left) was created especially to stencil on the wall around a picture frame or window. The addition of a bow, real or stencilled, would be a perfect finishing touch. The pretty little pinks can be repeated for a delicate all-over stencil. Just measure your wall and place the flowers at equal distances from each other, and you have instant wallpaper.

The daisy arch would make a very interesting border on the wall around a bedhead. Bedding could be stencilled to match. A lampshade or vase would benefit from the addition of the rose motif, or you could use it on writing paper.

Imagine the fat-petalled flowers (bottom left) stencilled on your bedhead or on a tablecloth with napkins to match. They would look equally good in either pastel or vivid colours. The little trailing bells look beautiful on drawer fronts, around a mirror or on a pretty lampshade. This is a dainty design to be used on small objects.

For a border full of movement, use the rose curl around a door frame. It would be very dramatic in red and gold or clean-looking in black and white.

The ever-popular honeysuckle will always look best in its natural colours. This design would be beautiful around the edges of a scalloped blind or tablecloth.

67

Chapter 6

PASTEL HUES

Ice cream sundaes and summer dresses;
marshmallows and milkshakes; pink
champagne and candyfloss; aquamarines
and lilac flowers. Every colour has its
pastel shade to soothe the soul and
calm the eye.

PREVIOUS PAGE This new shower room with its glass screen demanded a loose, airy design. Pale blue and pink flowers were cut in two sizes and stencilled free-style to tumble around the shower cubicle.

A stencilled clay pot and a stunning wisteria make a wonderful feature in this dining room.

Pastel colours are very pleasing to the eye and can be used to lighten a dark room or corridor. Just think of the choices available to you: cool, pale blues and greens; soft pinks and yellows; delicate lilacs and peaches. Because these colours are not over-powering, you do not have to stick to just one of them. A pale cream or white room would be the perfect canvas for a stencil design using them all.

A floral border of roses using a range of pastel colours would be terrific anywhere in the house. Stencil it on a wooden floor or on a sitting room wall to imitate a rose garden. You could also use rose motifs on a set of cushions with frills to match the flowers.

In contrast to a floral look, pastel checks in a kitchen or bathroom would be perfect, using lemon and blue or pink and grey. Or stencil pastel dots onto some of your kitchen tiles. You can vary both the size and the colours on different tiles for interest. Ice cream sundaes in pretty dishes would make an unusual border in a kitchen, too.

Design several different bird stencils for your bedroom, then make a motif for the wall over your bed composed of birds holding swags of pale flowers in their beaks. Repeat the bird design in the top corners of the room and place more birds flying around the walls and ceiling. Blue and grey birds with lilac flowers would be extremely pretty. Butterflies, too, can be made to flutter around your room in a collection of pastel colours. Use them in a border or stencil a group of them over your paintings and around your windows.

In the bathroom, grey and pink shells would be elegant on your curtains and as a ceiling-level border. Elaborate fish stencilled in mint-green, aquamarine and lemon would be relaxing. If you don't like fish, stencil seaweed or coral instead, using the same colours. A border of pale green fronds of maidenhair fern would look stunning, too, especially if you can stencil the sides of the bath as well.

If you have rooms or furniture painted in dark colours, do not worry. These will also be good backdrops for pastel colours, as the pale shades will stand out most effectively. Stencil shimmering white swans with pearlized paint onto a navy blue wall in your bathroom. Pale pink peonies on a black coffee table would be gorgeous, as would iridescent green leaves on a terracotta urn.

Bows are a popular stencilling theme. Use them over pictures on your wall or as a border in their own right, reversing your design at every second repeat. Bows are ideal as spot decoration on drawer fronts, dressing-table tops and door panels.

Strong geometric shapes can also be coloured with pastels, as the strength of the design will counteract the lack of depth of colour. The hallway of a modern house would be a good place to experiment. Try placing a geometric border at dado rail height, for example.

Picture mounts (mats) can be decorated to match any décor. It is best to keep the motifs simple so as not to detract from the picture they will eventually be surrounding.

In a dark stone recess built into an ancient fireplace, this tiny clock really glows. The delicate yellow flowers that surround its face took only 15 minutes to stencil.

Yellow is a marvellously cheerful colour with its association with sunlight and ripe crops. Creamy net curtains decorated with pale yellow daisy flowers would brighten even weak, wintry sunlight as it comes through your windows.

Screens are coming back into fashion and they are a perfect surface on which to stencil. Imagine a pale cream screen, its edges painted in metallic gold, with a delicate, soft pink rose clambering up the panels. It would be the most marvellous addition to any room. You can use almost any design on a screen, ranging from a border around the edges of each panel to a small landscape scene with hills, trees and river.

Another idea for using pastel shades is to stencil small boxes with different flowers in blue, cream and peach. You can keep jewellery, keys or sewing threads in the boxes. They would also make wonderful containers for tiny birthday presents to your friends and would be reusable afterwards.

Fans are always a favourite motif. A ceiling border of fans, each one with a pretty ribbon trailing from the handle, would be perfect for a young girl's room. You could vary the colour of each fan or each ribbon or both. Also, by varying the angle of the fan at each repeat, you will prevent the border from looking too static and give it movement. You could then stencil one large fan over the bed and put an extra decoration inside it, such as your butterflies. The addition of a matching motif on a cotton dressing gown would probably delight a young girl.

For a small boy's room you could stencil birds' nests with eggs of different colours in each one. Put spots on the eggs by stippling with the stencil brush. Here again, you would have a use for your bird stencils. Have the birds flying around, but this time put insects in their mouths. Pale ginger cats playing with coloured balls would be fun for small children, too.

In a sewing room, stencil bobbins of thread or balls of wool yarn near or on the work surface. A lacy border with tumbling ribbons would also look pretty and appropriate in this setting.

For a really original project, why not stencil a piece of silk and make a shawl for cool summer evenings? An ivory silk shawl with the palest turquoise and peach flowers, edged with a long cream fringe, would be a luxurious addition to your wardrobe. You could make a drawstring bag to match.

It is not difficult to find source material for pastel schemes. You can use absolutely any subject you want. All you have to do is to decide whether your chosen subject will look good in pastel colours. If you want your stencilling to be realistic, just think of pastel-coloured flowers such as apple blossom or Madonna lilies. On the other hand, you can choose subjects such as bows and ribbons that are not associated with any particular colour at all.

A summer straw hat, with imitation flowers and stencilled flowers inside and outside the brim. This idea works with fabric hats as well. Add ribbons or imitation fruit and tailor the decoration to match.

A pair of large-petalled flowers like those below would be delightful stencilled onto a cotton throw for a favourite arm-chair. The set of peony flowers and leaves forms another free-style stencil. Trace the individual shapes and see how many different borders and motifs you can make. The twisted rope motif can form an edging for floral designs.

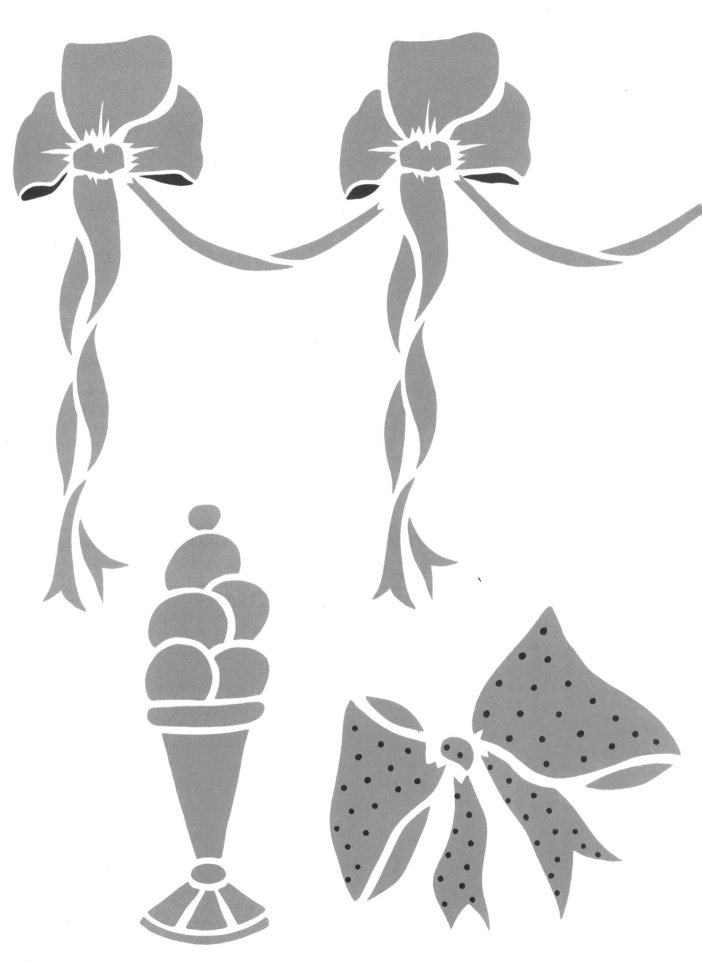

Colour the bow on the opposite page in pale pink and add the spots by painting them freehand in blue. Or try pale yellow with gold spots to decorate a little girl's room. The plain, twisted bow is also ideal for a bedroom and would look pretty decorating drawer fronts and wardrobe doors. Combine it with the hats border, giving the hats a change of ribbon colour at each repeat. Place the riband (opposite) at picture rail height to make an impressive border in a dining room.

Ice cream sundaes in pretty pastel colours would enliven a tray for summer drinks or a large umbrella.

The ivy-leaved toadflax shown below is a tiny lilac flower with a pale yellow centre. It looks very pretty and dainty growing out of cracks in the wall. So imitate nature and use the design as a motif on your walls, placing it all over to imitate wallpaper.

The snowdrops are ideal to stencil around the edge of a tablecloth and can be repeated on napkins. The tulips are a much bolder motif for a table mat or runner.

The tiny buttercup border was designed for picture frames, mirror frames and other such narrow surfaces. Stencilling of this nature does not shout out at you, but can be a fine finishing touch.

Chapter 7

LEAFY GLADES

*Pale new buds and glossy evergreens; red
and golden foliage tumbling in the breeze;
skeletal leaves pressed in a favourite book;
luxuriant greenery on exotic plants.
Leaves of all kinds are a visual feast of
colour and shape. Look around you on a
country walk or in a botanical garden and
you will find all the inspiration you need
for a successful stencil scheme.*

PREVIOUS PAGE *A garland of fresh green lemon leaves adds a hint of the Mediterranean to this handsome kitchen table.*

This dark, cool room has been enlivened by the addition of stencilled plants and leaves. They mingle with real plants to provide greenery at every level.

If you want a calm, relaxing scheme, you can do no better than to look at one of the many shades of green available to today's decorator. This is also the easiest way to bring the outdoors into your home. There are blue-greens, yellow-greens and brownish greens. If you really look closely at a country landscape, you will see just how many shades of green there are. An artist will mix a wide variety of greens to paint a landscape and it is the successful blending of these colours that gives realism to the finished painting.

The leaves and buds of spring are a softer, cooler green than the vibrant leaves of summer. Autumnal leaves are brown, gold, orange and red, forming a riotous panoply of colour to brighten the shortening days. Some leaves are variegated and can look stunning and life-like when stencilled onto your walls. There are leaves in many different shapes and sizes, too. There are long, sinuous leaves; sharp, spiky leaves; serrated or smooth-edged leaves; tiny leaves and large palm-like fronds.

To make your first simple leaf stencil, all you have to do is find a leaf that is pleasing to you in its size and shape. There is a vast storehouse of reference material in gardening books and books on botany. Perhaps the happiest way to track down your design is to visit the countryside or take

Stencilled ivy adds drama to a patterned glass uplighter and, as you can see, is especially impressive when the light is lit.

A plain coolie-hat shade is festooned with leaves to fit its surroundings. These delicate leaves make a strong contrast to the black base of the lamp.

a walk around your own garden. Just looking at your window-box could spark the imagination. Place your chosen leaf flat against a piece of paper and trace around it. Then simply transfer the design to a piece of stencil material and cut out the shape. You can make the stencil more interesting by repeating the same leaf at different angles or by using a variety of different leaves. The latter would give you the opportunity to use several different shades on the same border.

As I said, green is a very calming colour, even in its brightest forms, and is therefore ideal for use almost anywhere in the home. I am very fond of green in the bedroom and bathroom as these are areas where I can go to relax. So, how can you use your stencils? Small, delicate leaves look wonderful around a mirror or picture frame. You can imitate wallpaper by stencilling small sprigs of leaves onto your bedroom walls. Use the same design in a larger format in door panels or on lampshades. The small design can be used again on drawer fronts and around wardrobe door handles.

If you do not have a bedhead, you can stencil a headboard of leaves onto the wall. Palm fronds would give an exotic touch, while willow leaves would be more cottage-like. Stencil leaves growing from your uplighters and on your bed-hangings or curtains.

If you want to try something really unusual for a ceiling, start by painting it white and then sponging it in soft, pale blue. You can then stencil a canopy of leaves and branches onto this make-believe sky. This would be a marvellous treatment for any room, particularly for a bedroom or bathroom.

Alternatively, stencil ivy to tumble from the ceiling all around a door frame or window. Check your gardening books to see just how many wonderful variegated leaves you can choose from. Because ivy trails so beautifully, it makes a perfect floor stencil, especially in a hallway where it can carry on up the stairway and onto the walls.

Try stencilling a pair of large-leaved plants on each side of the doors in your hallway. This can look very distinguished. If you have a dado rail in any of your rooms, stencil a row of foliage plants in pots along it. This would give a distinctive touch to a dining room, for example.

A fireplace is an ideal focal point for your stencilled leaves. Use a mixture of greens, browns and ochres to outline the mantelpiece and fire surround. Stencil a floorcloth and perhaps a set of cushions to match. Plain glass lampshades can benefit from stencilled leaves in greens or autumn colours to make a glowing decorative feature on cosy winter evenings.

Another idea is to make circles of leaves such as laurel or bay. They are classic designs that would look good on a house sign, enclosing the house number or name. Bunches of stencilled herb leaves could adorn your kitchen cupboards. Or stencil sprigs of different herbs onto the drawers where you store the real thing. Circlets of spectacular autumn-coloured maple leaves could be stencilled at intervals along your hallway. They could also be added to the doors of a country cottage.

A conservatory is the ideal place for extra foliage. Stencilled leaves will provide a wonderful backdrop for your real plants and will help to fill in the gaps if you are just starting out. A really large ivy stencilled in one corner growing up from floor level to the roof would make a wonderful display. You could stencil ivy all around the room,

This leafy pot of lilies is very realistic. It stands as one of a pair on either side of the entrance to a library, adding a distinctive touch to the doorway.

just trailing down the wall from the ceiling. This would add interest to an area where there may not be enough light for real plants to survive.

You can make your leaf designs as simple or as complex as you like. A very simple shape can be made more interesting by the addition of veining. Do this by simply making an extra overlay and stencilling over the top of the initial colour. Look at the designs at the end of this chapter and you will see that there are many different ways to represent a leaf shape. I am sure you can think of more. You will also see that not all the designs are of an authentic leaf. Some are quite realistic, while others are more stylized. It is up to you to decide which style suits you best.

A contented ceramic cat snoozes high on a ledge amongst a trail of stencilled leaves. This is a free-style design that can meander anywhere around the house.

A striped effect is created on a plain wall by stencilling well-spaced vertical bands of a simple leaf design.

The trailing leaves on the opposite page can be made to meander along the floor and would look lovely wandering up a stairway. Try them in browns, russet reds and golden yellow. They would also be very effective as a backdrop to other plants in a conservatory. The large simple leaf border on this page (far left) can be used to great effect in a hallway or bathroom. You could colour the leaves in blue or bronze and clever shading will give them an extra dimension.

The small bunches of three leaves on the left would edge a mirror frame beautifully or make a bold statement if stencilled black on green in a bathroom, while the pretty swirly leaves below are a delicate motif to stencil all over your bedding.

The wavy willow leaves shown on these two pages will make a delicate border at dado height in a dining room. The geometric leaf border just above the willow leaves on the opposite page is much simpler, but would also make a stunning dado height border.

The leaf swag on this page could be added around the edge of a round table with the straight run of leaves slightly bent to fit the circular shape. The leaf and stem motif opposite would look distinctive on a lampshade or painted in different colours on kitchen storage jars.

The large ivy design on
these two pages was made
especially to tumble from a
wall light or a hanging
plant container. Use some
of the strands on the
container for added effect.
    The pretty little vetch
leaf is dainty and deserves
careful handling. Use it on
fine cotton voile at your
window and watch it billow
in the breeze. Simple oak
leaves and acorns would
look charming around a
door frame or to decorate a
rustic basket.

Chapter 8

CONFIDENT COLOUR

The flash of a kingfisher's wing; a stained glass window struck by sunlight; jelly beans and fields of sunflowers; sunset in the tropics and bright neon signs. Bold use of strong colours is the perfect way to make your environment more exciting and stimulating.

PREVIOUS PAGE These intertwining ribbons make a colourful border to brighten up an attic bedroom. Because the stencil is made up of a lot of single components, it can easily twine around doors and windows.

Masses of sunflowers like these would look wonderful as a feature on a chimney-breast. The simple border, if used around the room, would strengthen the decorative theme.

If you want to see colour at its most dramatic, you need only look at the natural world. The colours may be bright, but there is nothing in nature that jars the eye. Just think of some of the combinations you will find: the black and yellow of a bee; the red and green of a poppy; yellow grain against a blue sky; the mixture of colours in a rainbow. There are many, many more, so try to make a list of some of your favourites. This will form an ideal starting point in your search for a colour scheme. Of course, colour does not have to be bright and vibrant to be confident. Black and brown with a touch of cream as a highlight can look

very sophisticated, as can grey with white or silver alongside gold.

Now, where do you use all these wonderful colours? Some people can live in surroundings full of unrelieved, startling colour, although this would be too much for most of us to cope with. For them, any room in the house can be enlivened with brightly coloured designs.

A sitting room painted yellow with a bright border of sunflowers would be very cheerful and uplifting. Or stencil a bunch of large sunflowers over the fireplace. This colour scheme echoes that used by the artist Monet in the kitchen of his home at Giverny.

A deep green background paint is ideal for a Victorian hallway. Sinuous red poppies in the Art Nouveau style would complement this colour scheme perfectly. A study painted maroon with gold stencilled motifs would be very sumptuous, while a cream-coloured bedroom with purple and gold floral patterns on the curtains and bedding would give an elegant impression.

Orange and blue look wonderful together. Blue flowers with orange stamens or a series of coloured checks are both good ideas for a kitchen. A mixed border of kiwi fruit and oranges would also be bright and cheerful. Bright green, strap-shaped leaves intertwined with shoots of orange-red montbretia flowers would make a stunning border for a hallway. This plant has a wonderful shape where leaves, flowers and stems bend gracefully out from the centre. Try changing the colour of the flowers to other strong shades such as blue-purple or bright yellow for a different look.

Bright, colourful poppies decorate this mantelpiece. They will never fade and will attract bees and butterflies all year round. The fancy candlestick is one of a pair, but can be used just as well alone.

The clematis and peony border has been used as a single motif, then reversed to make a stunning floral arch over a chest of drawers.

You can make really pretty cushion covers using bright-coloured stencilling and co-ordinated frills.

Your bathroom is an ideal spot for experimenting with bright colours. Multicoloured tropical fish can wend their way around stands of glorious coral. Exotic birds can look down on the bath from their perches hidden in brilliant jungle flora. Of course, you do not have to decorate a room exclusively with these brilliant colours. Use a peaceful background of white or pale green as the perfect foil for splashes of colour. You can then use just one large piece of stencilling to make your confi-

dent statement. You can light it with spotlights or a picture light in the evenings to make it really stand out.

Stencils do not have to be restricted to walls. Cushions can be lavishly decorated with richly coloured flowers or birds can be stencilled onto lampshades using metallic or iridescent paints. A coffee table is the perfect place to stencil a really impressive and colourful central motif.

Monochrome stencilling can also work very well. Pick a colour, say blue, and within that framework select five different shades of blue. You may select kingfisher, duck egg blue, sky blue, navy blue and aquamarine. Use all these shades in one mixed floral border and then use single shades for individual motifs. You will be amazed at how effective this can be. Of course, you can try this with any other colour, and doing so will help you to build up your personal colour confidence.

For an unusual idea, try stencilling a border carpet in vivid colours onto a smooth wooden floor. If you then want to enclose the carpet design within a pair of straight lines, you can do this quite easily with masking tape. For each edge, just place two strips of tape along the floor, forming two parallel lines, and colour in the gap between them. Of course, you can make the stripe as wide as you like or make it a broken stripe.

For more colour ideas, visit some of the botanical or public gardens in your area. A good gardener must have excellent colour sense, as designing a pleasing garden requires the same principles of colour as interior design. You will find inspiration for both shapes and colours to help you make your stencils. Also, you can collect colour paint charts from art suppliers and do-it-yourself shops. Cut out the coloured shapes and use them like a jigsaw to see which colours go together the best. By doing this you will make your colour choices much easier.

You can really make a splash outside the house, too. If you use your garden as an extension of the house for entertaining and sitting out, you will probably have garden furniture. Deck chairs are usually brightly coloured and you can have fun adding your own stencilling to a plain fabric cover. Oversized flowers and butterflies are just two design suggestions. Add borders to large garden umbrellas and matching motifs to seat cushions. You could even stencil a special set of napkins for use outdoors. If you have large, plain terracotta pots on your patio, why not make some fun stencils for them? Bees or birds would be good subjects to try.

Stencilling onto dark backgrounds can be very striking. Dark blue walls with a set of stencils representing white doves in flight is a simple idea to dramatize a bathroom. In the end it will be your own personal colour preference that will prevail. As long as you are happy with the end result, that is all that matters. So be confident; select the colour scheme and start stencilling.

These floral tiles alternating with toning colour-washed ones make a bold statement and would look just as effective on the wall or the floor.

Use the pretty vase of poppies on a roller blind as a central display with the poppy motif (opposite) as a border. Poppy flowers come in all sorts of colours: bright red, orange, yellow, blue and pretty pastel shades. With these two designs you can co-ordinate a whole room. Use single flowers as simple motifs to provide variety.

The ornate candlestick is ideal for use on a wall just above a bedside table. The busy bee can fly around an open window or hover on your favourite honey jar. The butterflies and dragonflies are versatile designs. Group them around a bunch of real or stencilled flowers.

Clematis, peonies, buds and leaves make an elegant, curvaceous border to trail above a picture rail. This is a very versatile design as each element can be used alone or arranged to fit a certain space. Make a second overlay for the peony stamens and the clematis stripes.

Large, fat flowers cry out for bold colours. Use them on curtains or loose covers for your sofa or as a border around the floor. Exotic birds can walk along a conservatory wall or stand in opposing pairs over a doorway. You can make them really bright by using metallic or translucent colours. Either make a separate overlay for the eye or simply paint it in by hand.

Sunflowers are a great favourite. Use them as a border to brighten up your kitchen, then decorate your storage jars to match. Morning-glories can be stencilled around a doorway or inside a window area. They would also make a pretty motif for a T-shirt.

The interlocking ribbons make an unusual stencil. Trace the design and, by shading, see how many ways you can make the ribbons intertwine.

Chapter 9

INDIAN SUMMER

Tiger hunts and howdahs; intricate paisley patterns and the rainbow swirl of saris; exotic plants and ancient temples; jewelled knives and bright turbans; peacock feather fans and cool white dresses. India means many different things to different people.

India is a land of bright colours and patterns. Any book about the history of design will be sure to contain a large section devoted entirely to India. You will be able to find plenty of source material there for your own stencil designs. If you live in or near an Indian community, you will be able to get a taste of this fascinating country by just visiting some of the local shops. Look at the fabrics and see the kaleidoscope of colours on show. Examine the way the colours are used side by side. You will see lots of gold and other metallics used on sheer, filmy fabrics.

If you have a dark, dismal room in your home, why not cheer it up with some spectacular Indian designs? First of all, paint the walls cream and rag them using a soft plum colour. Then take up your stencil brush and make a border both at ceiling height and at dado height. Use gold, purple and green in an intricate pattern. Take elements of the design and use them as spot motifs between the borders. Next, take the same elements, enlarge them and use them between the lower border and the skirting board (baseboard). Although you will have used deep colours in your decoration, the room will look invitingly rich and warm.

Look at the architecture of India, especially the Taj Mahal. It is a marvel of curves and lines. I am certain that you could use it as the inspiration for many designs. The white of the building against a brilliant blue sky is a wonderful colour scheme for you to use, too. Many other buildings have beautiful domes and intricately carved arches that would lend themselves to stencil designs.

I am sure that most of you will be familiar with calligraphy. It is so adaptable, as the strokes can be used to make pictures as well as beautiful writing. Use Indian script in the same manner to make your own pictures or to make up fascinating, swirling designs. Just think of the wonderful colour schemes you could use as well. Blue and orange, green and gold, and blue and green would all be marvellous.

Take a close look at the peacock. This magnificent bird has the most glorious plumage from which you can take many designs. Use purples, metallic blues and greens for more realistic colourings or perhaps, for something different, use terracotta, black and brown. You could make a marvellous large stencil of a peacock for use on a screen or as a focal point in a sitting room.

Other wildlife of India can be the stimulus for your creative muse. A line of slate-grey elephants with brightly coloured canopy decoration could amble along a bathroom wall, interspersed with jungle foliage. This would be a perfect background for your collection of plants luxuriating in the steamy atmosphere. Crocodiles would be another fun subject for a bathroom stencil. You do not have to use realistic colours; try bright green or purple for a different and eye-catching look.

A plain mirror has been embellished with palm trees in metallic gold and translucent green paints.

*This tiger's head was
stencilled onto a piece of
silky fabric and some
bright green foliage added.
Elephants run around the
room at dado rail height to
make this a really
colourful corner.*

Tigers are almost synonymous with India and their coat patterns are simply beautiful. Make squares of tiger-skin patterns and use them in a border in your sitting room or make one large square to create an eye-catching point of focus over a fireplace in a modern home. You can use authentic colour schemes, but try using other mixes to match your décor. The bedroom would be another place to use your tiger-skin designs. Decorate your bedding and use the tiger's head stencil from the trace patterns on page 114 above your bedhead or on a wall hanging. Scatter cushions and mirror frames could also benefit from similar stencilling.

Look at natural history books for information on the fauna and the flora of India. There are many plants and flowers native to India from which you can construct your designs. Lilies are beautiful, popular flowers. They are very elegant and would be a welcome addition to almost any room. You could make them look exotic by using purple or red, peaceful and serene by using white and cream, or distinctly different with black flowers and gold leaves. Make them into borders, motifs, swags and circlets.

Use the same methods with another favourite Indian flower – the water lily. It often appears in Indian paintings, both in realistic and stylized forms. Bathrooms are the obvious choice for these flowers. Stencil them on the floor around your bath and on the wall around the mirror. Why not use them in the bedroom or kitchen as well? Stencil them in your bedroom as a low-level border along the skirting board and grouped in large motifs on the walls. In the kitchen, put them on the wall around the sink and in pastel colours on glass storage jars.

Orchids are another species native to India. They have unusual flowers in a spectacular variety of colours. A conservatory would be a good place to use them, perhaps as a backdrop to a small collection of real blooms. They would also be attractive grouped on the wall under a spotlight in your sitting room.

There is a wealth of Indian jewellery available in many places. It is intricate, often brightly coloured and offers great scope for the stencil designer. Turquoise and silver are frequently used and are great companion colours. Puppets and masks, too, are very popular in India. A row of different masks with varying expressions would make a very distinctive display in a hallway or study. If you copy your designs from authentic masks, try to stick to the original colour schemes.

To bring all your ideas about India together, you could make a wall hanging incorporating plants, animals and patterns, all with an Indian theme. Stencil your motifs onto silk and attach the completed hanging to a pair of gold-coloured rods.

You should find that a good travel book about India will be a first-rate starting point from which to get the feel for this wonderfully diverse country. You are bound to find one in your local library. Look at the pictures closely and you will be surprised how many design ideas will leap into your mind.

An inexpensive pine tray has been colour-washed in bright red and adorned with rich purple lilies. In addition to being useful, the tray would look wonderful as a decorative item displayed with some brass ornaments.

Try the oval lozenge shape enlarged on cupboard doors with another design inside. This and the rectangular lozenge can be used either horizontally or vertically. The palms would make an unusual addition to a conservatory, or could be used on a pelmet in a bathroom and also around the bath. The simplified turbans would be stunning in black and red on a gold-painted vase. The insignia design (left) can be used either way up. It would look particularly distinctive in a study or on a lampshade. Try working the dagger design into a circle to be repeated for a wall border.

The three-in-one design is very sophisticated and would look wonderful used as a dado border in a formal dining room or hallway.

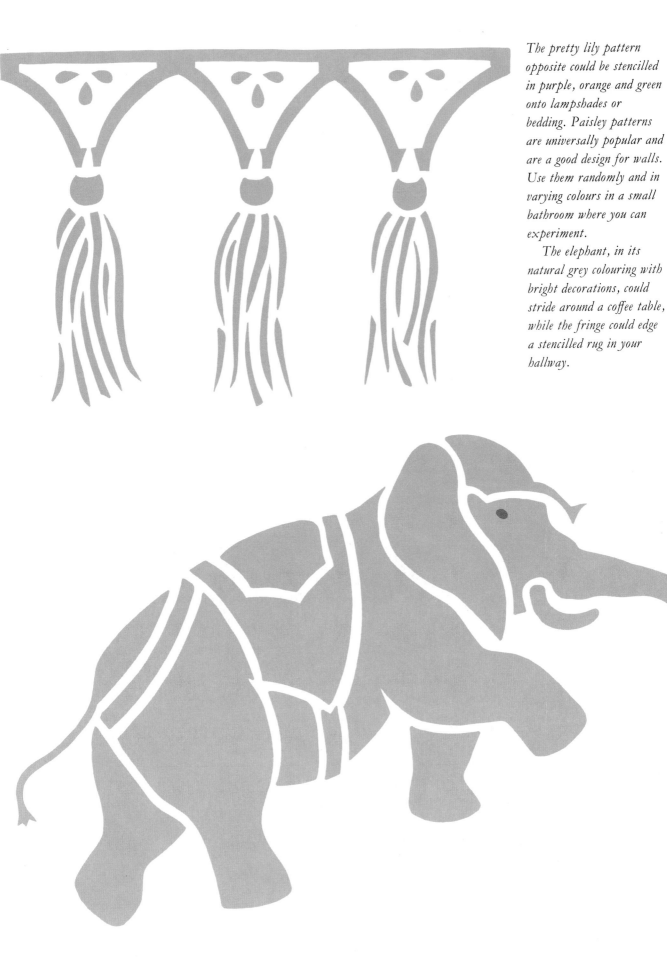

The pretty lily pattern opposite could be stencilled in purple, orange and green onto lampshades or bedding. Paisley patterns are universally popular and are a good design for walls. Use them randomly and in varying colours in a small bathroom where you can experiment.

The elephant, in its natural grey colouring with bright decorations, could stride around a coffee table, while the fringe could edge a stencilled rug in your hallway.

113

The tiger is a wonderfully strong subject. The design looks complicated, but can be cut in three parts. As a centrepiece for a coffee table or as a large motif over a fireplace, it would be unrivalled.

You will find that the other Indian-inspired designs on these pages have many uses. They are mostly shapes rather than recognizable objects. The dots and pod designs on this page are both wonderful border patterns. You could make changes by omitting certain elements as you go along and re-introducing them later. These designs cry out for bold, bright colours: gold and red, green and peacock blue, or purple and orange. The simple petals pattern opposite would be pretty around the edge of a silk skirt or around a bathroom mirror.

Chapter 10

NATURE'S HARVEST

*Nuts and berries; mushrooms and herbs;
seeds and rosehips. Nature is the great
provider. The sights, tastes and smells of
nature's bounty are a wonderful source of
ideas for your stencilling projects.*

PREVIOUS PAGE This plain new kitchen has been given a touch of distinction with a grape stencil, which has been used free-style around the room.

A beautiful treatment for an unusual feature. This cut-off pyramid shape is quite irregular, so the fragile blueberry stencil has been manipulated to fit. Purple and blue berries are stunning against the bright yellow background.

Try to imagine a profusion of berries growing wild in the hedgerows: shiny purple blackberries gleaming jewel-like against blue-green leaves; hips and haws in bright red, orange, salmon and yellow ready to feed the birds in autumn; wild strawberries appearing after the tiny white flowers to hide shyly under their leaves.

Probably the first place you will consider stencilling with this type of design is the kitchen. It is only natural to use them in the room where food is to be prepared. You can create a really bright colour scheme with borders of red berries. Run them along the walls between the worktop and wall cupboards, then stencil them along the edge of cream-coloured curtains and around the window frame. You can vary the size of the berries, small and delicate on the curtains and larger on the walls. For a more restful kitchen, use soft-coloured fruits such as peaches and apricots. Stencil a border on the wall at ceiling height and then trail the fruits down the walls.

Take a close look at the grape vine in the kitchen photograph on the previous page. This was built up using only the grapes and leaves from the corner motif on page 126. First of all, each element of the design (each bunch, leaf and stem) was cut out separately and in differing sizes. To make a realistic vine, the fruits and leaves were stencilled

onto the wall at varying angles and sometimes reversed. It was important to keep the directional flow to prevent the stencilling from looking haphazard. This is a perfect example of a truly adaptable stencil. Try this technique with other designs. If you are worried about building up a decorative feature in this way, you can practise first on a large piece of paper. Joined pieces of lining paper are ideal and inexpensive.

The kitchen is full of surfaces to stencil. Wooden bread bins, place mats, utensil jars and trays are ideal subjects, especially for the beginner. Of course, your kitchen cupboards are ideal for stencilling too. Each door will probably have a suitable flat surface, none of which will be very large and therefore not too daunting. If you make a tem-

plate of each surface using tracing paper, you can tailor your chosen design to fit. When you stencil a motif on one door, try reversing the design for the adjacent door. This will be more pleasing than having the same design all over. Don't forget, too, that you must measure and centre your designs so that the doors match. A swag of mixed berries and leaves would look absolutely stunning used in this way.

In the dining room, a garland border of crab apples would look welcoming combined with matching wreaths of mixed fruit. You could make place mats by stencilling onto squares of smooth pine, protecting them with several coats of varnish. This project could be followed up with matching drinks mats decorated with single motifs.

A small coffee table was colourwashed in a restful, pale green so that leaves in a darker green would stand out. The peaches are a mix of pale orange, mustard and grape.

This is my working sheet for the blackberry stencil on page 124. I will be making some new scented drawer liners for the winter, using marbled paper and this pretty stencil. Tied with ribbon, they are an unusual home-made gift.

A delicate border of blackberries would give a country feel to a cosy bathroom. Use purple, dark blue, pale green and soft reds to imitate the real fruit. If you have a hanging mirror, why not stencil a fall of berries on the wall around it? You can then work the design into a wreath for the walls. A set of four wreaths, each one representing nature's harvest from a different season, would look absolutely marvellous in a dining room.

Mushrooms, toadstools and wild grasses are all possible subjects for your designs and could look effective "growing" in small clumps at floor level near a back door. Herbs, too, are pleasing stencil motifs. They do not bear exotic flowers, but more than

make up for it with their varied and attractive foliage. A border made up of a variety of leaves from culinary herbs would be both pretty and elegant in a kitchen and would be an attractive supplement to bunches of dried herbs hanging from the rafters. This design would not be overpowering and could easily be carried into the dining room on seat cushion pads, tablecloths and napkins.

Don't forget the weeds either. Some of them, such as dandelions, have culinary or medicinal uses and deserve to be represented. Also, there are many edible flowers – nasturtiums and violets, for example. Combine several of them in a really pretty border that will create a talking point in your dining

A simple country doorway is warmed by cheerful rosehips and leaves in their autumn colours.

room, especially when you serve the real flowers as ingredients in a salad. Birds, animals and insects, too, all partake of nature's gifts and can be added to your projects.

You can use the alphabet stencils on pages 128 and 129 to add names to plants stencilled onto herb jars. Alternatively, stencil the herbs and their names onto the kitchen floor, each within its own square. In this way you can build up a make-believe tiled floor.

In the sitting room you could stencil garlands of hops to drape around your fireplace or over doorways. Heads of grain are another suitable subject and you will find many traditional designs to choose from. Wheat or barley can be stencilled in wreaths or stacks onto doors and floors. You can mix a few poppies into the grain, if you like, for added interest.

For inspiration and reference material, look in natural history and cookery books. There are also many books on gardening that would be invaluable. For an authentic historical look, you could do no better than to seek out some old illustrated herbals. They have relatively simple illustrations that you can adapt for stencilling. If you come across books specializing in wreath-making, you will find these worth their weight in gold. As for colour schemes, you may want to try to be as realistic as possible. Alternatively, many of these designs could be stencilled very imaginatively with metallic paints.

This delicate camomile bunch can be stencilled onto dark walls for extra impact or enlarged among other, real, dried flowers. The bundle of rosehips can be repeated as a border or used as a motif on cupboard doors.

Try stencilling the mushrooms onto tiles in subdued colours. You could also use them in your child's room down at skirting-board level, but this time use all sorts of bright colours.

The squirrel with the acorns is an appealing design. Cut the motif quite small and have him standing on any of the rosehip and berry borders. It will be fun for your children to try to spot him as he gathers his winter food store.

The large rosehips and leaf motif would look splendid around a kitchen fireplace. Use reds, yellows and burnt orange for an autumnal look. Use the juicy blackberries on the seat and back of pine chairs or make seat pads and matching place mats.

The dandelion is a useful medicinal plant. Stencil it onto dark tiles and just stipple the "clock" with white paint.

Colour the dainty berries in blue and purple on your bedding or use a bright shade of red for a richly stencilled hallway.

Grapes are a very popular motif. This design would look elegant as a corner piece around your dining room door. Paint green, black or purple grapes or make mixed bunches in all three colours. Imagine bright strawberries or golden ears of wheat running along your kitchen wall just above the tiles and repeated on câfé curtains.

Make two overlays for the peach stencil so that you can colour the crease in a darker shade to make the stencilling more realistic. Then use the design just below ceiling height in your kitchen. Oranges and lemons are simple fruits, but can be an exercise in shading to produce a realistic look.

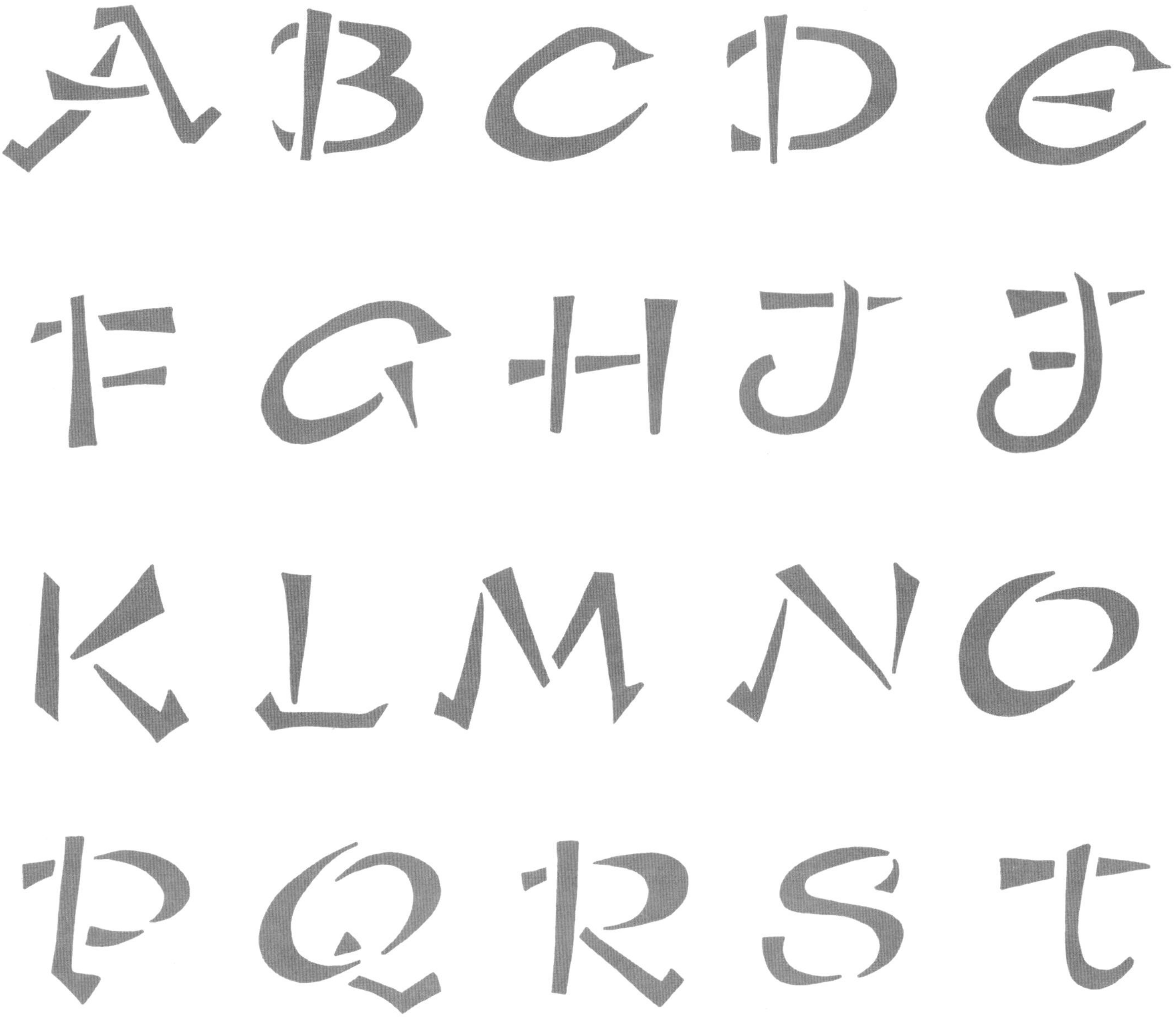

A B C D E

F G H I J

K L M N O

P Q R S T

There are many creative uses for these two alphabets, which are quite different in style. Spell out your child's name over his or her bed; design a name board for your home; make personalized greetings cards or monogrammed luggage. You can also use the alphabets to add lettering to T-shirts, handkerchiefs and stencilled samplers. There really is no end to their possibilities.

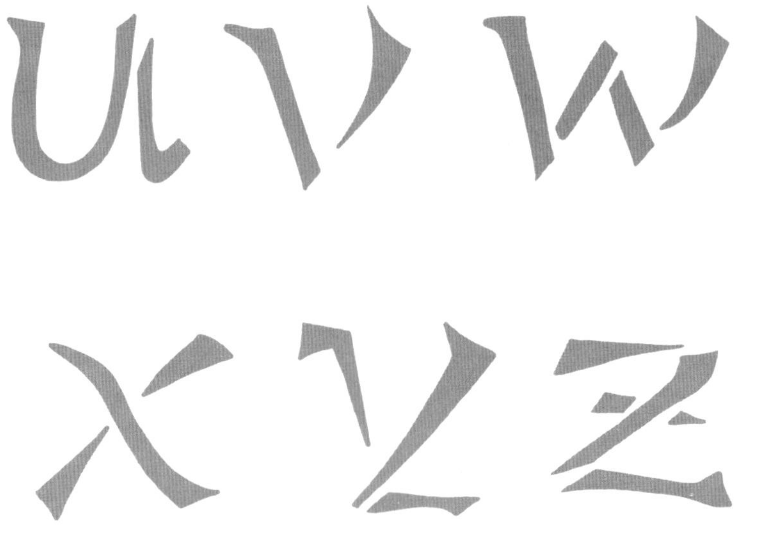

U V W

X Y Z

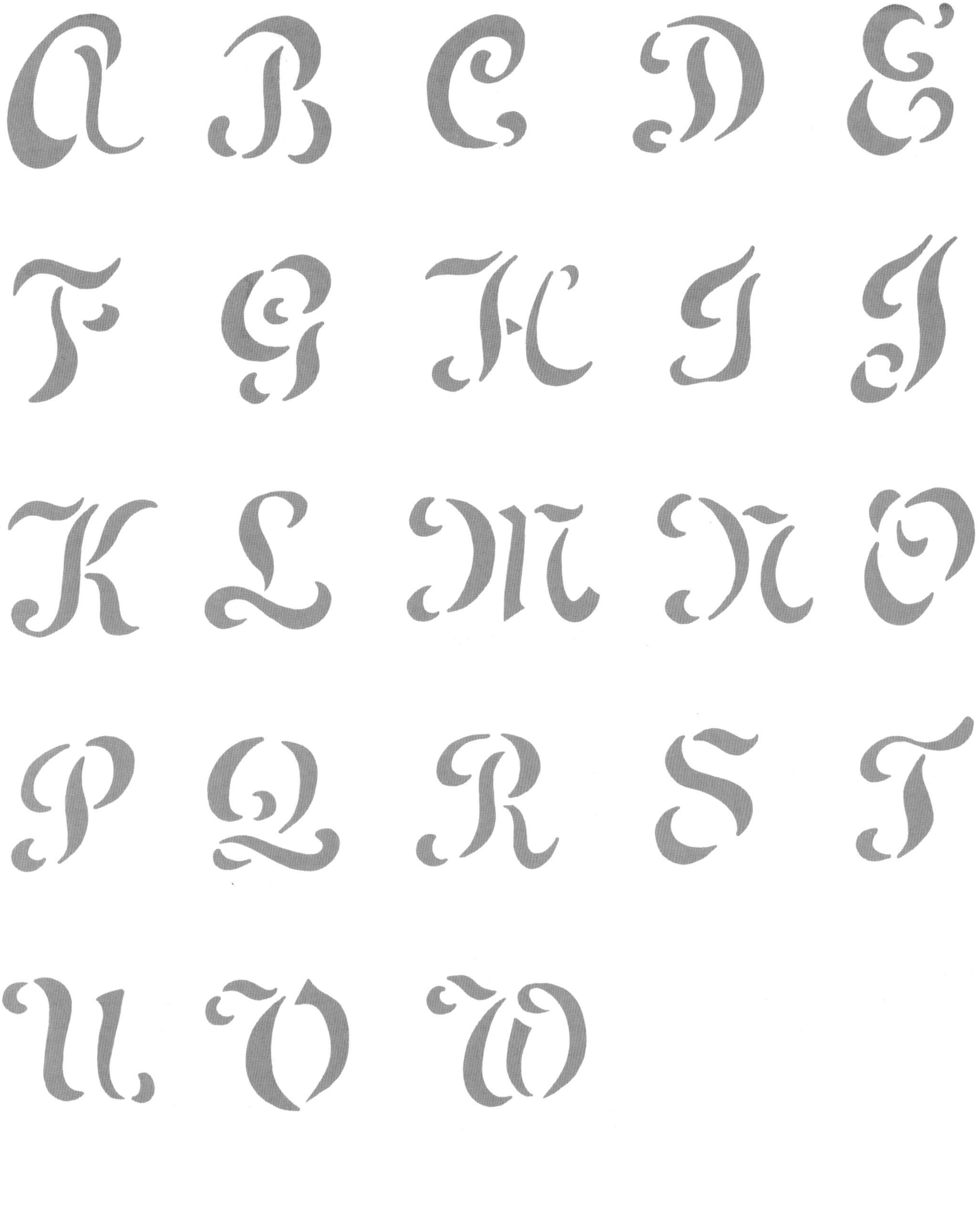
A B C D E
F G H I J
K L M N O
P Q R S T
U V W
X Y Z

MATERIALS
AND TECHNIQUES

WHAT IS A STENCIL?

A stencil is any paper cut out with holes or 'windows' through which you can paint colour onto a chosen surface. The stencil can be as simple or intricate as you wish, from a design on a single sheet, or overlay, used with just one colour, to several overlays using many colours.

Each part of the stencil has a role to play. The holes form the pattern and the spaces between, called bridges, or ties, separate the different elements and give a sense of realism and depth to the design.

MATERIALS

CARD: The most traditional material for making a stencil is manila card. This is a heavy-gauge card that has been soaked in linseed oil to make it waterproof. Ideally it should be used with oil-based or spray paints, because water-based paints will eventually make it soggy and unusable.

The advantage of using manila card is that it is easy to cut. Its main disadvantage is that you can't see through it, which is important when you line up your design for a repeating border, or a design comprising more than one overlay. The answer is to cut registration marks into the stencil or notches into the edges of the stencil, which can be matched with each overlay. Alternatively you can simply select one or two elements of the design and cut them out of each overlay. But remember to only paint them once.

ACETATE: Draughtsmen's acetate is the best type for stencilling. But always choose the right weight for the job. If it is too stiff it will be difficult to cut and won't bend around corners easily; if it is too thin it will tear. Acetate is shiny on one side and slightly opaque on the other. It is long-lasting, easy to clean and you can see through it for easy registration. Draw directly onto the opaque side of the acetate with a pencil and paint onto the shiny side, but remember that the image will be reversed when you turn the acetate over. Wipe your stencil clean from time to time to prevent a build up of paint in the windows.

PAPER: Providing you are not going to put your stencil to extensive use, you can make it from heavy paper or cardboard. Both are easy to draw on, easy to cut and have the added bonus of being inexpensive. However, unless you use heavy tracing paper, you will not be able to see through your stencil for registration purposes.

METAL: Stencils made from thin brass are long-lasting and easy to clean, but you can't see though them for registration and they are difficult to cut.

OTHERS: You can use a piece of lace or paper doilies to create a pretty stencil and interesting, if delicate, effects on walls and furniture. A few coats of varnish will strengthen them long enough for limited use.

You can create very unusual effects with a finely cut stencil. The vase shapes on this planter give an intriguing trompe-l'oeil impression.

EQUIPMENT

BRUSHES: It is easy to recognise the traditional stencil brush by its round stock and flat-cut bristles. It's a specialised design which hasn't changed for centuries. You can buy brushes in a variety of sizes, each one designed for a particular task. The largest brushes, with the biggest stock, are suitable for floors and those stencils with larger windows in their design. The smallest brushes are for the tiniest details. I prefer to use the largest brushes possible, as they seem to blend the colours so much better.

As stencilling continues to increase in popularity, brushes and other tools of the trade are readily available from art supply shops and specialist stencil stores. If you have difficulty in finding stencil brushes you can use an ordinary paint brush, but unfortunately they are not so adept when you're blending colours. It is also possible to use an old shaving brush, but you must cut the bristles flat across the top. Do not use an expensive brush as the bristles will be too soft.

Be sure to clean your brushes throughly when you have finished work. If you look after them they will last a lifetime.

SPONGES: Try experimenting with a sea sponge to apply the colour. This will give a beautifully dappled effect to your stencilling. And a mixture of brushed and sponged stencilling on one project will add texture to your chosen design.

PAINTS: If stencillers of bygone days could see the selection of paints and the range of colours available today they would be positively green with envy!

You should have no trouble at all in finding the right paint in the right colour for whatever project you have in mind. You can use many types of paint for stencilling, depending on the effect you wish to achieve. All you have to do is match the paint to the surface, whether plaster, wood, fabric or glass, and use common sense. For example you should always use non-toxic paints in children's rooms.

ACRYLICS: These are available from all good art supply shops and come in a wonderful array of colours, including pearl and metallic finishes. They are fast drying and can blend easily. As acrylic paints are water based you can thin them with water, and you can clean your brushes quite easily afterwards with warm soapy water. The fast drying qualities of acrylics make them ideal for stencilling.

As stencilling requires very little basic equipment, it is worth investing in a good cutting utensil and brushes. The surface to be decorated will dictate the paints to be used.

STENCIL PAINTS: These are also water-based, but are normally sold in pots and are more liquid in form than most artist's acrylics. As they are specially made for stencilling, they are very fast drying so you can get on with your project much quicker. Brushes may be cleaned in warm water.

OIL PAINTSTICKS: As the name suggests, this is oil paint, but it is specially formulated into sticks that look like chunky wax crayons. They are very easy to use and the colours blend beautifully. As the crayons are 'self healing' they do not dry out and will last for simply ages. The only drawback is that, as the paint is oil-based, you will have to clean your brushes with white spirit before washing them in soapy water.

CREAMS: Stencil paints in cream form are a new addition to the range of paints available to the stenciller. They are a solid paint in a jar so you can hold them in your hand while stencilling and just dip in your brush when it needs reloading. Cream paints are suitable for use on all surfaces including fabric.

SPRAY PAINTS: Many professional decorators use car or other spray paints for stencilling. They are available in a large range of colours including metallic. No brushes are required as you just spray the paint directly on to your chosen surface. More often than not you can use just one overlay, as the wonderful effects are obtained by subtle use of the spray. The great disadvantage of spray paints is that they can be very messy, so you must protect surrounding areas with newspaper to stop the paint spreading. They are also quite difficult to use until you get the pressure on the nozzle just right. Do not be discouraged by all this as the final results can be quite stunning.

FABRIC PAINTS: There are many different makes of fabric paint available which can be used in the same way as acrylics and other water-based paints. Many can be fixed by ironing or by tumble drying. You can stencil onto most fabrics but natural ones such as cotton, linen and silk are the best.

CERAMIC PAINTS: These paints are for use on tiles, pottery vases, tableware and other ceramic items. Unless you have access to a kiln, only use those paints that don't need firing. Bear in mind that these paints are for purely decorative purposes and, as such, will not stand up to a lot of washing or the dishwasher. So don't think about decorating the dinner service just yet!

JAPAN PAINTS: These are oil-based paints which are also extremely fast drying, making them perfect for stencilling. The range of colours, however, is not extensive.

OTHERS: You can use any kind of paint for stencilling as long as you match the paint to the surface. Beautiful effects can be achieved with watercolour paint; however, this should be thickened by mixing with a little acrylic paint. I often use it un-thickened on heavy watercolour paper and let the colour bleed. Not very traditional, but different!

All water-based household paints can be used but they often take too long to dry, which can be a disadvantage if you are trying to decorate your room with a multicoloured border or frieze.

Wood stains and varnishes also give interesting effects. You can obviously use them on wood, but clear varnish mixed with a little oil paint can be quite beautiful as a decoration on glassware.

Always follow the manufacturers' instructions. Some paints, as well as solvents, can be dangerous!

As you become more confident you will be able to stencil large images, floors and ceramics with ease. Although the designs in this room are all quite different, their colours are reflected in the patchwork tablecloth.

PREPARATION OF SURFACES

As with all forms of decorating, the surface must be prepared to accept the paint you have chosen. If you don't do the groundwork, you will not get good results. Dust and grit under the stencil will prevent it from lying flat and make the paint bleed under the stencil paper.

WALLS: Remove all traces of old wallpaper and fill in any holes. It's not necessary for walls to be perfectly smooth; it all depends on the look you want to achieve. Allow newly decorated walls to dry out thoroughly before stencilling. You can stencil onto bare plaster, but treat it first with clear universal sealant.

PAINTED SURFACES: You can paint onto virtually any painted surface providing it is properly prepared. Gloss paint must be 'keyed' by sanding first. You should not have to seal your stencil with varnish unless it is to receive heavy use. Varnish the whole surface, not just the stencilled area as varnish tends to yellow slightly with age.

WOOD: Remove any wax or varnish and strip off old paint using a proprietary stripper following manufacturers' instructions. If the surface is very rough, sand it first with a coarse sandpaper, followed by a 'wet and dry' sandpaper to give it a final smooth finish. Don't forget to always paint with the grain.

GLASS: The only prerequisite here is that the glass should be clean, dry and free of grease.

FABRIC: Fabric should always be prewashed to remove any trace of dressing and then ironed. The dressing can cause the paint to bleed and ruin your stencilling.

WOODEN FLOORS: Using coarse sandpaper then grading down to a 'wet and dry' sandpaper, sand the floor, with the grain, to give a 'key'. When you've finished, vacuum and wipe down with a lint-free cloth. For an old floor, you may have to use an industrial sander to get a smooth surface and to get rid of any old varnish and polish. Sand the corners and edges by hand. When you have finished stencilling, seal the floor with at least two coats of colourless varnish and your work of art will last for years.

METAL: Remove old paint using the correct proprietary stripper. Remove any rust with a wire brush and sand the metal with steel wool. Stencil directly onto the metal or paint first with a metal primer. Oil based paints are best to use on metal as they help prevent rust; remember to seal your stencilling with a coat of clear varnish.

CERAMICS: Ensure the surface is clean, dry and free from grease, then stencil directly onto the surface using ceramic paints. Again seal with a proprietary varnish to give your work a longer life.

PLASTIC: Before stencilling always 'key' the surface with fine sandpaper. You can also paint the plastic first, then stencil onto the paint.

PAPER: You can stencil onto most types of paper, although a textured wallpaper is not an ideal surface as it will break up your design.

LINING UP

The following instructions for lining up your stencils are guide lines only. You can position a border with great scientific precision, only to find that it looks rather odd in a room that is not perfectly square.

CENTRE POINTS: All you need are two pieces of string. Pin the end of one piece of string in one corner and pin the other end in the opposite corner. Repeat the procedure with the second piece of string in the two remaining corners. The place where the strings cross is your centre point.

VERTICALS AND HORIZONTALS: To find the true vertical of a wall you will need a plumb line. Coat the string with chalk and attach the plumb line, fairly high up, on the wall. Let the plumb line settle. Then, holding the plumb weight steadily against the wall with one hand, 'twang' the string. This will leave a line of chalk on the wall.

A spirit-level and a ruler or a tape measure are all you need to find a horizontal line. Decide at what height from the floor you want your stencil. Measure this height at intervals along the wall with chalk or a soft pencil. Then attach a piece of string to the wall at both sides so it runs along the marks and draw in the horizontal line.

BORDERS AND FRIEZES: Always begin in the middle and work outwards. You may find that the design will fit the space available using the exact number of repeats. If the design almost fits the space, you can stretch it or compress it slightly as you work, but if there is just too much space left over, you can take some of the elements from the stencil and make a corner motif.

ROUNDING CORNERS: You may find it easier to treat each wall individually and use a corner motif on each one. This method works rather nicely around a door frame, putting the corner motif at the base of the frame and again at the top corners.

An acetate stencil will bend into a corner and you will be able to carry on stencilling without interruption. Don't forget that if you are stencilling a border around a whole room, your design will have to join together at some point, so be prepared!

MITRING CORNERS: Draw a pencil line at 45 degrees into the corner. Then put a strip of masking tape against your pencil line and stencil up to the tape. Move the masking tape to the other side of the pencilled line and match the stencilling into the corner. As this can be tricky, always do a dummy run on a piece of paper before attempting the real thing.

MOTIFS: You can place motifs on the wall or floor in a random manner using your eye as a guide. You can, if you wish be more precise and draw up a grid. To do this, simply attach one end of a piece of string to the centre of one wall, at floor level, and the other end to the centre of the opposite wall. Mark the position of the string on the floor, move the string an equal distance along the two walls and make the next set of marks. Continue until you have all the lines you need and then repeat using the two remaining walls. Now you can place the motifs as desired.

STENCILLING TECHNIQUES

To fix your stencil to the wall you can use low-tack masking tape positioned along the outside edges of the stencil. This will keep it secure, but won't remove your paint surface. Alternatively, you can spray the back of the stencil with spray adhesive. This also holds the stencil in place, but allows you to peel it away from the surface and reposition more easily. Always use in a well ventilated room.

APPLYING THE PAINT: The best advice I can give you is to practise your stencil on a piece of paper first. The other golden rules are always to use a dry, clean brush, and never to overload it with colour as this will cause the paint to seep under the edges of the stencil paper and smudge the design. A dirty brush will taint your colours.

USING PAINT STICKS: These have a 'sealing skin' over the surface to prevent the paint from drying out. To obtain the colour and break the seal, simply rub the point of the stick onto a separate piece of acetate. Pick up the colour on your brush by rubbing it gently into the paint, using first a clockwise and then an anticlockwise movement. Hold your brush at right angles to the stencil and apply the paint using the same circular strokes. Always start by applying the paint around the edges of the cut-out areas first. This will create a lighter area in the middle, as the colour is worked off, and is the first step in shading your design.

USING STENCIL PAINTS: Don't use the paint straight from the pot or tube because you will invariably overload your brush. Put a little of the paint onto a saucer and, if necessary, thin down with the appropriate thinning agent to get better consistency.

Dip the brush into the paint, wetting only the ends of the bristles. Now take most of it off again on a paper towel or newspaper by rubbing the bristles gently clockwise and then anticlockwise onto the paper. When your brush is practically dry, apply the paint gently to the stencil, again using the circular movements. Begin painting at the edges of the cut-out areas, working to the centre to give a shaded effect.

USING FABRIC PAINTS: Make sure that your fabric is laid out flat, with a layer of absorbent paper underneath as some lightweight fabrics will allow paint to seep through. This is the one occasion when you can use a damp brush because the fabric will absorb a lot of moisture.

The procedure now is exactly the same as for water-based paints. However, I recommend using spray adhesive to hold the stencil in place as you will not be able to remove any paint that seeps under the edges.

USING CERAMIC PAINTS: When applying this paint it is better to use a stippling motion. Hold the brush at right angles to the stencil and, by flexing your wrist, make a gentle dabbing motion with the brush onto the cut-out areas.

USING SPRAY PAINTS: Practise with the spray paints before you commit yourself to your project, as it takes some time to produce the gentle 'whoosh' that indicates the pressure on the nozzle is just right.

Hold a piece of cardboard, as a guard, at an angle against the part of the stencil you are trying to paint and spray towards that. The paint will just drift onto the stencil and the windows will not become clogged. You need just the lightest film of paint with each coat.

If you use a stencil with a single overlay you may get some overspill from one colour to the next, but sometimes this creates beautiful effects.

SHADING: While it is perfectly acceptable to stencil with simple colours, say green for the leaves and blue for the flowers, you will get a much more professional effect if you add shading to the design, giving it realism.

Shading can be added merely by putting colour on the outer edges of the pattern, leaving a paler area in the centre, rather like a patch of sunlight. You can also get a similar effect by painting lightly all over the design in one colour, then adding another, stronger coat around the edges. Several different colours may also be used for shading. For example, when shading a blue flower, I'll also add a hint of purple to the shadow area. Where a leaf curls behind a flower, the flower colour can be used to shade the leaf. After all, this happens naturally! So, if you stencil a complex pattern, don't worry if some of the colour spills over into other parts of the design.

CUTTING YOUR STENCILS: Use a new blade in your knife or scalpel for each stencil and change it regularly. A blunt blade will rip your stencil rather than cut it cleanly. Put your stencil material on the cutting base and place one hand on the acetate or manila card to keep it steady. Take the craft knife or scalpel and make firm, smooth cuts, always toward yourself but away from the hand steadying the stencil. Cut each window in one stroke for the cleanest edge. Always begin at the centre of the design and work outward, cutting the smallest windows first. If you cut the largest ones first, the stencil will lose strength and subsequent cuts may tear the bridges. Leave a border of about 2ins (5cm) around the cut-out pattern to stop paint spilling over the edges.

MENDING DAMAGED STENCILS: Just put a strip of masking tape over both sides of the rip and simply recut that area.

When starting a new stencil, take the first colour and apply the paint lightly to the surface, in this case the leaf area of the design.

With a clean brush apply the second colour, using the same technique.

Create interesting shading by applying a third colour to give depth and realism to certain areas of the design, for instance, under the leaf or on the outer edges of petals.

Finally, apply the fourth colour, again using a clean brush.

STEP-BY-STEP INSTRUCTIONS

Trace your chosen design either from our trace patterns or from a reference book onto good-quality tracing paper, using a soft pencil. If you are cutting your stencil in acetate, trace the design directly onto the non-shiny side of the acetate. Remember the image will be reversed when you stencil as you always paint over the shiny side of the acetate. To avoid image reversal, place the design under glass and the acetate on top of the glass. Cut the acetate following the lines visible through the glass.

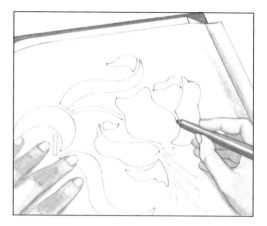

If the design is not the right size for your purposes, you may need to reduce or increase its size. To do this take a sheet of tracing paper drawn with a squared grid, then trace the design. Take another sheet of grid paper with either smaller or larger squares, as required, and copy the design square by square onto the new grid.

If you are making your stencil from manila card, you will need to transfer the traced design onto the card. Do this by rubbing the reverse of the tracing paper with a very soft pencil. Then place the tracing paper, right side up, onto the card and rework the outline using a hard pencil to transfer the image onto the card.

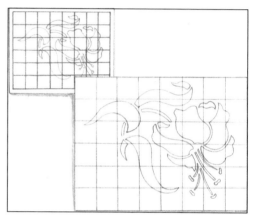

To cut a manila card or acetate stencil simply lay the acetate or card on a sheet of glass (with the edges bound in masking tape to prevent accidents) or on a self-healing cutting board. Using a new blade and scalpel or craft knife, cut out the stencil using firm, smooth cuts. Always cut toward yourself but away from the hand holding the stencil. Cut each window in one stroke for the cleanest edge.

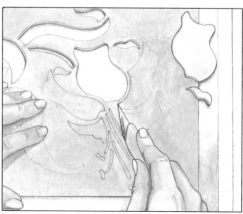

Position the stencil onto the surface you are decorating. Secure with either low-tack masking tape or spray adhesive. The latter helps you reposition the stencil several times without damaging the surface, so is probably more helpful for beginners. Always use in a well ventilated room.

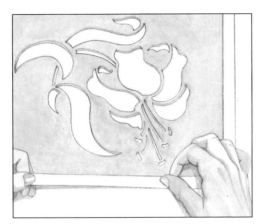

Apply a little paint to a dry brush. Work most of the paint off the brush on to a dry paper towel or newspaper. It is much better to apply the paint in several thin layers rather than in a single thick one which will only cause the paint to seep under the stencil paper and smudge your work.

Holding the brush like a pencil in one hand and supporting the stencil with the other, apply the paint to the cut-out areas of the stencil using light circular movements, in both clockwise and anticlockwise directions. Build up the colour and shading gradually.

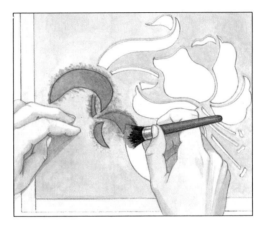

When you have completed the stencil, gently remove it from the surface. Using the registration points, reposition on the surface and continuing stencilling until you have completed the required length. For simple designs you can reposition the design by eye only. Clean away any build up of paint on the stencil as necessary.

If you have more overlays for additional colours, position each one in succession over the stencilled area. Again use the registration points. You should not have to wait long before using additional overlays as most stencil paints dry rapidly. Always remember to use a clean brush for each new colour.

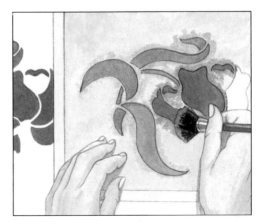

CREATING DESIGNS

These are examples of what you can achieve with just one simple motif. I made the single tulip motif and decided to see how many other designs I could create with it. As you can see, there are nine more designs shown here and it was only lack of space that made me stop. See if you can find any more.

Enlarge some of the motifs and mix them back in with the smaller ones. This will change the look of the design enormously. You could also square off the motif by taking away the curves and replacing them with straight lines.

Now trace some of the designs and try colouring them in with coloured pencils. Make a monochrome border; then try green leaves with yellow, red or pink petals. Next, try a set of motifs with flowers in mixed colours. Try to use unusual colours such as gold leaves and black petals. Playing around with designs in this way will teach you a lot about the art of stencilling, and will enable you to develop both your design and your colour sense.

INDEX

ACKNOWLEDGEMENTS

I would like to thank the following people for allowing us to stencil and photograph in their homes: Anna and David Fitton, Beverley Martin, Tania and Steve Lewis, Rhona Platt, Linda Fox, Carol Kidger, Barbara Williams and, last but not least, John and Karon Meehan.

A special thank you goes to my husband who has given me inspiration, support and wonderful photographs. I could not have produced this book without him.

The author and publishers would like to thank Lizzie Orme for the pictures on the following pages, which are styled by Linda Barker: 37, 44–45, 61, 80–81, 85 and 131.

GLOSSARY

US readers may not be familiar with some of the terms used in this book.

UK	US
bath	bathtub
blanket chest	wooden trunk
blind	window shade
candyfloss	cotton candy
card (stencil)	cardboard
corn	wheat and other grains
cushions	throw pillows
doilie	doily
dressing gown	bathrobe, housecoat
fitted wardrobe	built-in closet
frill	ruffle
ladybird	ladybug
loose covers	slipcovers
net curtains	glass curtains
pelmet	valance
picture mount	mat
skirting board	baseboard
throws	afghans
writing paper	personal stationery

Many people in the U.K., have lent us props and merchandise for which we are very grateful:

Panduro Hobby,
Westway House,
Transport Avenue,
Brentford,
Middlesex TW8 9HF.

Orchard Trading Co.
Walkley Clogs,
Hebden Bridge,
W. Yorks.

Scartop Country Pine,
Spring Mill,
Bury Old Road,
Heywood,
Manchester.

Janet Harrison,
Heywood.

Daisies,
1 Whitehall Street,
Rochdale.

Harriet & Dee,
7 Police Street,
Manchester.

Boots the Chemist.

LIST OF SUPPLIERS

ENGLAND
Elrose Products Ltd.
20/21 Heronsgate Road,
Chorleywood,
Hertfordshire,
WD3 5BN.

The Stencil Store,
91 Lower Sloane St,
London SW1 W8DA.

Stencil Decor,
Eurostudio Ltd.
Unit 4,
Southdown Industrial Estate,
Southdown Road,
Harpenden,
Herts. AL5 1PW.

Lyn Le Grice Stencil Design Ltd.
Bread Street,
Penzance,
Cornwall TR18 2EQ.

The Stencil Library,
Nesbitt Hill Head,
Stamfordham,
Northumberland,
NE18 OLG.

AUSTRALIA
The Stencil House,
662 Glenferrie Road,
Hawthorn,
Victoria 3122.

U.S.A.
The Stencilers Emporium,
P.O. Box 536,
Twinsburg,
Oh 44087.

Stencil Artisans League Inc.
P.O. Box 920190,
Norcross,
Georgia 30092.

S.A.L.I. is a friendly, non-profit making organisation whose members work to promote stencilling throughout the world. Members are kept up to date with all the latest products and techniques.

144